THE MARRIAGE You Always Wanted

But Never Thought You Could Have

ED ANDERSON

WHOLESOME READING DISTRIBUTED BY:
CHOICE BOOKS
IRWIN, OHIO 43029
We Welcome Your Response

Except where otherwise indicated, all Scripture quotations in this book are from the Holy Bible, New International Version, Copyright © 1973, 1978, 1984 International Bible Society. Used by permission of Zondervan Bible Publishers.

Verses marked KJV are taken from the King James Version of the Bible.

The Marriage You Always Wanted But Never Thought You Could Have

Copyright © 1988 by Harvest House Publishers
Eugene, Oregon 97402

Library of Congress Catalog Card Number 87-083231
ISBN 0-89081-655-7

All rights reserved. No portion of this book may be reproduced in any form without the written permission of the publisher.

Printed in the United States of America.

*To my wife, Margaret,
whose intimate heart has
made this book possible.*

INTRODUCTION

We were told to get ready for the worst. The yard had been cleared of lawn furniture and toys, doors and windows were locked shut. Masking tape spanned x's across the large windows of our lakeside home, adding strength to each glass pane. A hurricane was coming. We had finished preparations. Little else could be done except to ride out the storm and hope our preparations were adequate.

We could have ignored the National Hurricane Center warnings and saved ourselves the trouble of extra work. After all, we could have reasoned, the storm center might not hit us squarely anyway. Why upset our schedules and prepare for something that might not happen? But, that reasoning would have resulted in a needless risk.

Marriages can experience hurricane-like forces strong enough to damage or destroy frail marital bulwarks. There is always the threat of an uncontrolled storm on the horizon. What can a couple do to preserve their marriage from icy stares, slamming words, sarcastically sunny smiles and rainy wet blankets before the height of a storm leaves everything ever treasured in shambles?

Giving up on a marriage is easy. Staying married is not so simple. A petty disagreement may cause the erection of defensive walls that cannot hold against the storm of difference—of opinion, of background, of understanding. As the walls shiver under the blows and frenzied patching, the two people behind them become more bewildered, enraged and afraid.

Every couple will experience hurricanes during their years of marriage, but they will respond to those storms according to the strengths and weaknesses inherent to their relationship. Those who have prepared for storms will have a far better chance of surviving than those who have not. Preparation for eventual difficulties and problem-solving skills for identifiable existing problems can begin with this book. *The Marriage You Always Wanted* was written to help you cope with and strengthen your marriage. The results of that effort are in your hands.

Part One examines the people, common experiences, spiritual dimensions, frustrations and joys with which nearly all married people can identify. I believe most couples are looking for heart harmony, but they often encounter far less than their idealized dreams. The potential for romantic reward is a latent theme in Part One and is further expanded in Part Two as the why's and what's are complemented with a series of how-to's.

Those of us who are married need to employ the best principles, techniques and attitudes to bring honor to our marriages and to our Creator. It is my prayer that *The Marriage You Always Wanted* will provide you with the biblical insight, psychological observation and inspiration to assist you in your quest for marital excellence and satisfaction.

— *Ed Anderson*

CONTENTS

Introduction 5

Part One

1. Three Couples 11
   A Montage
2. The Dating Game 19
   Mysterious Lint and Quick Turns
3. The Intimate Connection 27
   *When Chocolate Truffles
   and Fresh Roses Are Not Enough*
4. Time and Time Again 45
   How Much Time Is Intimacy Worth?

Part Two

5. Nine Seasonings to Savor 61
   Loving Is an Affair Every Day, Not Everyday Fare
6. Communication 85
   Collision or Consensus?
7. Discovering Differences 93
   A Not-So-Trivial Game
8. Out on a Limb for Your Mate 107
   A Case for Vulnerability and Trust
9. Sez Who? 121
   The Seven Steps to Conflict Resolution
10. The Love You Need 131
    And the Conflict You Cannot Resolve Alone
11. Hot, Cold or Ho-hum 143
    What Does Sex Have to Do With Intimacy?
12. The Salvation/Love Ratio 165
    Salvation Is to Baptism What Love Is to Sex

Notes 173

PART ONE
You Have the Potential for Heart Harmony
(The What's and Why's)

CHAPTER ONE

Three Couples
A Montage

*P*ushing against his collar, an artery pulsated with rhythmic joy. Bob's hands held the steering wheel gingerly, as if it were made of hot, buttered French bread just out of the oven. A song formed in his mind, and he offered up a guttural sound, naming the woman of his choice. Something irridescent, an intense warmth, grew in Bob's eyes until they gleamed. The corners of his mouth stretched into a sagacious smile. He was thinking of his Roxanne, could not get her out of his mind.

He was in love and boasted of it, sometimes secretly yelling to the sky above his delight in her love. Now he was on his way home. Today was special—their fifth wedding anniversary.

At home, Roxanne was picking up the odds and ends scattered throughout the bungalow, eagerly anticipating Bob's arrival. She had made plans. She had centered her whole day upon this moment. Early in the morning, she had reached for his hand to awaken him, and his response had gently caressed her mind all day.

She knew how he delighted to do special things for her, but this morning he completely surprised her. Somehow he had arranged a bouquet of flowers on the dresser without her noticing. A fancy, frilly new gown decorated the closet door, his favorite perfume (and hers, too!) tucked in its pocket. After she wrapped herself in the luxurious gown and lavished the fragrance on her throat and wrists, Bob lifted her in his arms and carried her into the dining room. He had prepared a sumptuous breakfast, beautifully arrayed on their best china. The silverware had been polished to a mirror shine, and fresh, red roses graced the table.

"Oh, Bob! How? When?"

On the wall, a banner declared Bob's love. A card on top of a half dozen giftwrapped presents reaffirmed his commitment to her. It was a time to remember.

Knowing that Roxanne did not have to be at work until one o'clock in the afternoon, Bob had arranged to take the morning off. After breakfast, they leisurely talked about their five-year marriage, the up's and down's, the good and bad times, even the time when they had talked about separating.

How is it possible that this couple, who love each other so dearly now, could ever have thought about breaking up their marriage? But for a time, Bob and Roxanne thought that divorce was the only solution to problems they apparently could not work out. So what happened? How did all this romantic stuff come about?

If I told you it was because of hard work, you might put this book down right now. I hope you do not. Let me assure you that there are many components to a successful marriage, not just hard work. But frankly, nothing you can do will accomplish the goal unless you are willing to apply all your energy and resolve to the principles in this book. That is where the work comes in. Do some thinking with me. Allow yourself to be challenged and inspired.

Bob and Roxanne's marriage is stronger than it might have been if they had not mastered a crisis together. Another couple, Janet and Doug, have yet to discover how much they need each other.

Janet watched her husband through the kitchen window. He slammed the garage door and nervously checked his wristwatch. A few moments later, obviously attempting to be casual, Doug announced that he wanted a quick, painless divorce. Janet had sensed this might happen but could not see how she could prevent or hold it off, yet his announcement shook her. Thirty-five years old and a mother of three, she had sacrificed much to be a good homemaker and companion to her ambitious husband. She knew that he had made sacrifices, too, but what had gone wrong?

Doug's words echoed in her mind for days. Could they ever recapture the relationship they had in courtship and the first year of marriage? She thought of the afternoon when Doug gave her the lovely, delicate, perfect engagement ring that would never leave her finger. Nothing, not even a late-night flat tire on the freeway could dampen their spirits then. When their first baby came, they were more in love than ever. Was the love affair really over?

Doug's responsible position at the company and Janet's responsible mothering at home had split their attention. Exactly when it happened, this parting, neither knew. Doug vaguely suspected it had something to do with his personal aspiration to be the best that he could be—no holds barred, no matter who or what was in the way. Janet mused that perhaps, just perhaps, she had overreacted to Doug's stubborn professionalism that isolated his time and attention from her and the children.

Things kept getting in the way, too. The car was one of those things. Janet had always thought the upwardly mobile wife should drive a station wagon, have a pedigreed sheepdog and at least two model children. Of course the car had to be paid for. Even the dog cost more money than she had anticipated. Shaggy Mortimer III came with impressive papers even if he did have one or two unimpressive habits. The house was another *thing*...not that Doug and Janet particularly wanted to compete with the Joneses or be ostentatious. They did want to own something a bit out of the ordinary even if it entailed a thirty-year mortgage, high monthly payments and stiff taxes. Janet completely redecorated and furnished the fifteen-year-old structure to make a personal statement. It may be Doug's castle, but it was her domain, she thought. Admittedly, credit cards had tempted her to overspend, not too much, but the monthly payments were beginning to tighten the family budget. Laura needed braces, and Tommy was clamoring for a baseball glove and shoes. Emily wanted to be a Brownie. It was enough to make any mother sigh. And now Doug.

Doug remembered how Janet had spent hours, even days, making herself beautiful for him. He had looked forward to their dates. Every one of the times they spent together had had a novel quality to savor. The wedding had been a bit of a bore, but the following days and months had been pure delight. Now, after ten years, some of Janet's sparkle was gone. She was exhausted when evening arrived and the children were finally in bed. When Doug timidly approached her for attention, she would mumble something into the pillow (he could never quite catch what she said) and fall asleep. Doug had grown used to watching late-night television, then stumbling off to bed, irritated that morning meant another day of too much pressure and far too little enjoyment.

After thinking it over, he decided he had taken enough neglect. Now was a good time to call it quits. Janet could have the car. She could have the furniture, too. He wondered uneasily how they would share the children. But there was one thing he could not do, and that was mention his loneliness and discouragement.

"No," Janet thought, "this is not the time to

give up. Our life-style is going nowhere, but not everyone's is. There has to be an answer out there somewhere." A divorced girlfriend gave her the name of a Christian marriage counselor and as much advice as she could give over three cups of coffee and an omelette. After that, Janet patiently worked on Doug to get him to go to the counseling center with her. He was reluctant, convinced that a decision made ought to be a decision kept. But he was curious, too. Who knows, the relationship might turn around if Janet could learn where he's coming from. A counselor might get her to see his way of thinking. Doug was curiously pleased to think that Janet was concerned enough to initiate doing something positive about their relationship.

Then there are Jim and Terri, who have been married for four years. Like others, they lost their starry-eyed idealism long ago but avoided confrontations. Neither could pinpoint the exact issues, but this morning their unspoken truce exploded. Jim wonders if Terri will ever allow him to touch her again. He is still bewildered by her verbal slap, "Your touch is not only unwelcome, it's repulsive! If you love me, leave me alone." Jim realizes that their sex life had always revolved around his needs, but Terri had never protested, never rejected him before this. She says she cannot take his exploitation any longer. Exploitation! The guilty thought that maybe he was never enough of a man to meet Terri's needs runs relentlessly through his mind. Jim and Terri need help.

Of the three couples, two have problems, different and yet alike in one respect: They lack intimacy. Wouldn't you think that couples, and especially newlyweds, would want to spend as much time together as possible? Instead, couples often abandon their commitment, sometimes even before the honeymoon is over. They allow their hurts to tear them apart. They neglect their relationships...and for what?

Intimacy takes two. God has designed a set of marriage principles, a solid foundation for healthy, enduring intimacy. If we respect God's judgment, we will not leave pastoral protection at the wedding altar until we are sure that what we want is what God wants for us.

Pop counselors, sage hens and even scholarly, scientific researchers have filled bookstore shelves with "fail-safe" cures for the marriage blues. Some say that marriage is outdated, an insult to the autonomy of the individual. In an age when carnal needs are fastidiously catered to, the self-discipline to achieve marital intimacy is a radical departure from the norm.

The rewards of real intimacy—not the fabrications of video screen soaps—far surpass anything that the pleasure-seeking imagination can devise. Two human beings communicating intimately elevate themselves to a godly plane, to freedom and enjoyment others cannot experience. God created husbands and wives to be intimate partners. You will see. With His help, you have the potential to create the marriage you always wanted but never thought you could have.

CHAPTER TWO

The Dating Game

Mysterious Lint and Quick Turns

*I*n the humming coolness of the air conditioner, oblivious of the scrambling downtown traffic outside, Janet fretfully reflected on miscellanea, the irritating little episodes and fears that had somehow gotten out of hand. A frown traced across her face, and she caught her breath. "Before we were married, David was anxious to talk to me. No one had ever been more transparent. We were close then. What a difference marriage made!"

I have heard so many variations of this story that I doubt if King Solomon, with his hundreds of wives, could have come up with a new slant. Women like Janet are often left with nothing more than disappointed dreams and uncertain futures, unable to understand their husbands' behavior. Their husbands, when explaining themselves, make excuses that amaze me every time I hear them. Why cannot everyone experience intimacy of the sort that brings about satisfying relationships?

It is possible to accomplish marital compatibility. The rewards are for those who earnestly and patiently strive for them. True intimacy is costly. It is not for the faltering and weak. It is for robust lovers who are full of zest for life and who choose to follow God's plan.

"Love is Blind"

The axiom is an old one and often referred to... with good reason. Early in the stages of friendship, many of us assumed that we had already developed a strong, intimate relationship when we experienced a captivating euphoria. At that point, we tuned out the rest of the world and concentrated on the emotion that overwhelmed us. Although we were unaware of what we were missing, we lacked the balance needed to maintain a stable relationship.

Years ago, most cars came with bench seats, front and back. This was a boon to romantic dating couples. Slick, slippery, translucent plastic seatcovers provided a means to closeness. The young man would usher his date to his waiting automobile (the family car entrusted to him by Dad) and see to it that she was comfortably seated before closing the door. As he strolled around the rear of his vehicle, he would glance through the window to see where she had chosen to sit. (Most young ladies positioned themselves midway between the steering wheel on the left and the passenger door on the right so as not to appear too aggressive and yet not communicate lack of interest, either.) That way he could guess what potential the evening offered. The closer she sat to the steering wheel, the less challenge she posed.

After the social event was over, a short drive into a dimly lit area was the usual tack. But how does a guy head for the city limits without alarming his date? He uses distraction, clever conversation and an air of innocent ignorance about the direction his car is traveling. If the lady shows little alarm at the absence of street lamps, he can feel fortunate.

After driving a few miles out into the country, he would contrive, in the dim light of the instrument panel, to spot a piece of lint on the seat between the two of them. After casually flicking the lint off, he would drop his hand to the seat. If he were lucky, his date would also spot a piece of lint and rest her hand beside his but not touching.

Then, twirling the barney knob of the steering wheel with his left hand, our 1950's teen makes a quick right turn. Gravity and those slick seatcovers are in favor of this move. His hand is pressed to the seat to keep it from moving while his date's hand and warm body slip toward his until their hands touch. Now the fireworks begin, pulses quicken and the world holds fresh promise. Neither acknowledges this phenomenon even though their intertwined hands communicate a new and delicate intimacy.

Both enjoy the exhilaration of the moment—they are on cloud nine.

Wait. There is more. Most 1950's-vintage cars were outfitted with standard-column shift, posing a problem for the young male. He would have to find a long, clear road to avoid unnecessary shifting; otherwise he could not drive with his right arm on the back of the seat. But wouldn't you know it? There is another piece of lint, this time on the back of the seat. Will she hesitate and move toward the door if he removes the lint and rests his arm behind her shoulders? She allows it! Minutes later his arm has begun to ache in its immobile position, but then a stop sign appears. He has to downshift the car, and the magic moment is gone.

Did they experience intimacy? The euphoria felt like intimacy to them! That is the point. The warm feeling was no more than a quick sensation. Feeling-oriented relationships require neither knowledge nor understanding—just the warm emotion you have when you see a person you want to touch, to talk to, to be with. Is this the intimacy that will last to a sixtieth wedding anniversary?

What I have described to you as a first date is what tricked many of us into thinking we were "in love." In fact, we were just starting out on a long, delicate and arduous journey into the soul of another human being that might, only might, bring about the results we longed for. We could not be in love until we learned to *know* each other, really *know* each other.

The first attraction that causes temporary emotional unity resembles a narcotic effect. We may be so driven by the need to satisfy our craving for each other that we suspend good sense and even good manners. Romances such as that are intense from the beginning. It is not difficult to imagine, then, why the relationship develops jealousy, perplexity and the fear of rejection.

Beginning relationships typically depend upon appearance, personality and charm, and not one of those characteristics will build a substantial friendship. Fantasy intimacy dissolves into boredom when preoccupation with each other is replaced with dollar concerns, daily work schedules, housekeeping, having babies, cultural differences and social pressures. These are the ordinary activities of life, yet they must be adapted to with tenacity, integrity and balance. If not, simple irritations will become threats. If the touch that once launched your soul heavenward has turned into a revolting sweaty palm and calloused grip, you are probably in the crisis of marital disillusionment.

The English poet and essayist Joseph Addison commented caustically, "Beauty soon grows familiar to the lover, fades in his eye and palls upon the senses." If intimacy is based on *appearance, personality* and *charm alone,* the natural result will be cynical disillusionment. Those three fascinating qualities can be produced synthetically almost at will. They have all the flavor of the theater. But if intimacy is based upon thorough knowledge, the natural reward will be honest communication and resilient personal commitment.

Rare is the individual who selects a date on the basis of integrity and compatibility. Usually, the real person is discovered only after the initial flow of heart heat has begun to subside and the head has cooled to a refrigerant level. It is too bad, too. Many bodies contain tender, beautiful human spirits that have been neglected because they are considered physically unattractive, are socially uncultivated or are uneducated. It is a wonder that a marriage could survive this first, fleshly evaluation once the romantic veneer has worn thin!

Cessna Aircraft ran a short advertisement to publicize its fixed-price pilot training program:

Cessna will make you a pilot for $2990. *Guaranteed.* [1]

Soon after the ad appeared, the company received this letter:

Dear Cessna,

In response to your ad in the latest *Popular Mechanics*, we would like to order a pilot for $2990. The following particulars should be built into your design: male—quick learner; height six feet, two inches, to six feet, five inches; weight 190 pounds; chest 46 inches; waist 34 inches; shoe size 11—optional; hairy chest and muscular; dark blue eyes; wavy brown hair.

We see by your ad that this pilot is guaranteed, but we would prefer to take him on approval. We have several other people also interested in your pilot program. Could we get a discount on case lots?

Although the letter was written in jest, it is not too far from real-life experience after all. But, it does not have to be *your* experience. You can have a healthy marriage by learning to hear and be heard, to know and be known. In successful marriages, people know their mates very well. They do not pretend they know. They actually do know—and not only hat sizes or preferred brands of chocolate, but the details that reveal feelings and values, the stuff of life, the hopes, dreams, fears and pain. That information does not come simply or easily. It takes effort.

CHAPTER THREE

The Intimate Connection

When Chocolate Truffles and Fresh Roses Are Not Enough

So then, what is this *intimacy* that is at times so hard to achieve? The word means something different to everyone. I believe it refers to three primary levels in progressive degrees of closeness. The first level of intimacy is a warm friendship that has developed over a long period of time. The second is where two friends freely share their deepest thoughts and emotions with each other. The third relates to a relationship of a very private nature. Of course, having a conception of *what* intimacy is and can be is not the same as knowing *how* to develop and maintain it.

Unfortunately, intimacy is not always the desired goal of a relationship. Some of us avoid even the thought of intimacy because it stirs up anxiety and insecurity, of exposure to deep-seated thoughts and feelings that we have tucked away behind buttressed walls. Walls constructed to secure us from embarrassing emotional revelations. Walls that have successfully deflected inquiries into their contents. Walls that stand in smug defiance of any attempts to penetrate them. Walls that create a safe haven. Intimacy could be threatening.

Others see intimacy as an exercise in which physical parts flex to achieve a mutually satisfying response. They refer to this as having sex, supposing that their bodies harmonize simply because they *are* intimate. To them, sexual intimacy is the major reason for the marriage relationship. If their sexual relationship fails, they consider their marriage a failure. If they are sexually satisfied, they cannot imagine a better marriage.

But sex does not guarantee intimacy. A five-year-old was staying with her grandparents while her mom and dad leisurely whiled away a second honeymoon in the Bahamas. To see if she had any idea what was happening, her grandmother asked her, "Honey, do you know where your mom and dad are today?" She replied innocently, "Grandma, don't you know? They're vacationing in the pajamas!" To some, vacationing in the pajamas is a pleasant thought, and they would consider it an opportunity for genuine intimacy. It might stir the imagination...it might even cause one to lose concentration! Yet, sex does not create intimacy; it is one symbolic result of an intimate relationship.

To others, intimacy is soft music and a bear rug, or it is good conversation over a delicious meal. Others insist that it is two lovers staring at each other for a long time. Whatever, concentration is necessary if you hope to discover and appreciate the richness of intimacy. You have to give your mate your full attention. The more you look at and listen to and consider your mate, the more you will appreciate and enjoy his or her company.

God Modeled Intimacy in Creation

These bodies of ours that react and interact are remarkable pieces of workmanship. God created the body machine as a tangible proof of His sovereign power, intellect and creativity. God's innate awareness of His entire creation—including you and me—is another phenomenon reflecting His awesome power. To fathom something of God's supremacy, imagine cataloging the intricacies that make up the human body. Isolate and synthesize the values, feelings and interests that generate a personality distinctly original among the billions of souls created since time began. Listen to their pleas for help, all the while alert to the dynamics in play that blend the course of God's creation with His will.

Then consider God's creation of a man and a woman. When God created Adam, He dug into the earth, incorporating its elements to form flesh and blood into a living body. He handcrafted every bone, sinew, corpuscle and muscle. He skillfully shaped Adam's personality and abilities. Eve He tenderly formed from Adam's ribs. God created a man and a woman in His own image—with will, mind and emotion—and gave them a rare gift, the power to choose their own destiny. God never left the humanity He created. He interacted with men and women down through the ages. One day He sent His Son to pay the ransom that enabled them to experience eternal intimacy with Him in heaven. Then at Pentecost, God sent His Holy Spirit to guide, comfort and empower every believer, present and future, in a personal, intimate relationship unlike any that had ever been experienced.

From the dawn of creation, God has paid close attention to His creation. What kind of response has He received in return? On the day that Adam and Eve took the serpent's suggestion that they could become like God themselves, the intimate connection was broken. They became anxious and ashamed.

Ever since then, God's intimate knowledge of both outer and inner human space has challenged mankind's tenacious desire to be independent, to be powerful, to be selfish. The kind of intimacy God wants runs counter to our natural inclination to withdraw selfishly into ourselves. Any marriage will be threatened by the rift developed by selfishness. Selfishness stops cold any effort to create or restore closeness. It sounds something like this: "I want what is best for *me*"; "I want that car"; "I want that woman"; or, "I want that toy." Being selfish means giving your mate's needs scant, if any, consideration.

Selfishness is sin. When we feel insecure and

selfish, afraid of our own vulnerability, we try to control others. The desire to wield supreme power is a need born of insecurity. A Christian must deal with personal selfishness if only for the reason that Jesus predicted, "Whoever tries to keep his life will lose it, and whoever loses his life will preserve it" (Luke 17:33). By His standard, selfishness is self-defeating.

The selfish desire for power over other people is seductive. Former U.S. Secretary of State Henry Kissinger called power the "ultimate aphrodisiac." Many are driven by it. In a *Wittenburg Door* interview (December 1985), bestselling author Henri Nouwen was quoted, "People who are afraid are interested in power, whereas people who are in love are always willing to give up power."

Do you make a concerted, unselfish effort to know and understand your mate as God knows and understands you? "Through him all things were made; without him nothing was made that has been made. In him was life, and that life was the light of men" (John 1:3,4). God has intimate knowledge of everything, but we have to learn how to become intimate. It is not a "given." Many will never know what intimacy really means. Our natural inclination is to hide, to cover up as Adam did in Eden. Adam worried that what he knew about himself would be revealed and he would be discredited in God's eyes. The first man had to learn to trust God even when punishment and self-revelation were inevitable. We must do the same even when repercussions might be unpleasant. Clear vision and trust are necessary for intimacy.

God gently but persistently encourages us to give Him our attention and accept His guidance and care. As a couple are drawn closer to God, they are drawn closer to each other (see diagram). A marriage that includes a healthy spiritual connection is potentially stronger and more intimate than it could ever be without that connection.

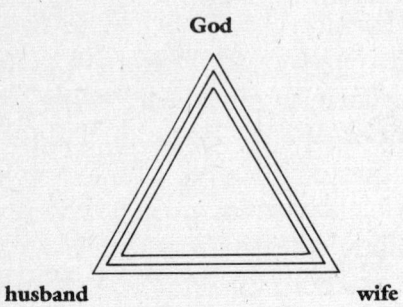

God Modeled Intimacy in Communion

The first-century Christian bore ridicule and repulsion when demanded to explain the symbolic, sacramental nature of the Lord's Supper that not only commemorates Christ's death and resurrection, but looks forward to His return in triumph. Rumor that Christians drank the blood and ate the body of their risen Lord shocked the sophisticated Near Easterners. They supposed that Christians were reviving the drunken, bloody rites of ancient mystery cults. Gossip halted the Christian celebration in public, and many Christian fellowships went underground to share the misunderstood, sacred love feast.

With the initiation of the Lord's Supper, Jesus' followers realized that He intended to have an ongoing, intimate relationship with them. The act of closeness was to be practiced regularly. "For whenever you eat this bread and drink this cup, you proclaim the Lord's death until he comes" (I Corinthians 11:26). Through communion, God regularly reinforces the intimate, honest relationship that began at creation. The same honesty and purity apply to communion with your mate, and especially to that special, most intimate of personal encounters.

When the Intimate Connection Is Broken

I could tell you story after story of people in pain and panic who wanted to have their marriage relationship rescued instantly after neglecting it for years. Unless we guard our marriages like royal caretakers guard England's crown jewels, we risk losing an irreplaceable treasure. "Be self-controlled and alert. Your enemy the devil prowls around like a roaring lion looking for someone to devour" (I Peter 5:8).

To establish a healthy marriage, you have to *care about* and *take care of* your partner. That means giving and accepting loving attention. From the first moments of birth to the last moments of death, all of us contend for attention. As we mature, we develop increasingly sophisticated ways of capturing and holding attention. If we repeatedly deny a loved one's need for attention, or if we are denied ourselves, a bleeding emotional gash will short the channels of communication and intimacy. The emotionally famished partner may deny the wound, but it will fester and spread unless it is cured with love and understanding. The why's of an emotional wound are not always apparent, but they need to be understood if you hope to help your wounded mate.

Let me tell you about George. His story is not uncommon. It is one of a severed intimate connection.

George, you understand, was a model son. His parents took pride in his public role, and they intended to ensure that the image he projected was impressive and consistent. They regimented his activities, his goals and his behavior.

It was essential to George's parents that he behave "correctly," no matter what the cost. The cost was at George's expense, of course. He learned to smile on cue. He dutifully practiced his spelling and arithmetic. No motivation could have been stronger than his doting and determined mother. He recited the capitals of the United States to his very-concerned father at the dinner table. If he did well, he enjoyed a friendly, approving atmosphere; but if he stumbled and stuttered and became flustered, he soon lost his appetite.

George's regimentation was well-meant. It was to prepare him for adulthood; but it had another aspect, too, since it showed what high-caliber parents he had. After all, his accomplishments were products of their sacrificial efforts. George was to carry on the family name, and in comparison to that responsibility, his personal desires were relatively unimportant. What counted most was loyalty to his heritage and veneration of his parents and grandparents whose gilt-framed portraits were carefully arranged on the piano in the family room.

Unknown to most, fear reigned at home. You would never believe it if you had not looked into it for yourself. The house was rather old but well-kept, its oak floors gleaming with buffed polish, its lace curtains starched and bright, big bouquets of fresh-cut flowers from the garden adorning the magnificent, dark-walnut buffet and coffee tables. There was no material want there. George's father was on the town council, a likable sort of man. George's mother was warm and affable. She enjoyed chatting with the neighbor ladies over a cup of coffee. Only one thing was wrong, and that was George.

No matter how he tried, George could not meet his parents' standards for him. You see, they were young once, too, and they knew kids' tricks to avoid responsibility. George had to learn to do what was right and like it. Before long, George gave up any attempt to assert himself. Gradually he doubted his own creative potential and simply struggled to be an extension of his parents. But, frustrated with his less-than-perfect performance, George became depressed.

Early on, he feared authority figures. Then, as a teenager, his fear turned into anger. Instead of draining his energy as fear had, anger created energy. Anger was refreshing. He found that he could direct its energy to accomplish his own goals and devise ways to deal with people who he thought posed threats to his personal freedom. His newly acquired size and muscular strength contributed to a better self-image, although he occasionally resorted to belligerence to assert his fractured sense of masculinity.

In the course of several thoughtless meanderings in and out of education and careers, George met a young lady who consented to marry him. At first, George felt relief from the compulsion to please his parents. He bragged about his weight lifting and amused his wife with tales of his prowess and daring during his high school years. All he needed to do was please his wife, a simple enough task, he thought.

Complications increased in geometric proportion to their years of marriage. Because of an intrinsic lack of confidence in his own judgment, George vacillated on almost every issue, purchase and decision. Time and again his wife intervened to relieve him of distressing burdens and responsibilities. He coped so poorly with stress that she tired of being his sounding board and took on the challenges herself. George was glad to be rid of the responsibilities, but he resented his enterprising wife and complained at the slightest provocation. To maintain a semblance of happiness at home, she did everything she could to please him.

George thought her life was full enough. She color-coordinated his clothes, pressed them and laid them out for him every morning. She did the laundry, bought the groceries, did the cleaning. She handled the family budget (somehow she always managed to make the money stretch), wrote all the checks, figured out the taxes. She took the cars in for regular tune-ups and repair. She mowed and manicured the lawn and shrubbery, and she maintained a prize vegetable and flower garden. She pickled cucumbers and prepared strawberry preserves. She attended the women's Bible study at church on Thursday mornings. What more could she want? Surely not to know him better, to desire more of his personal attention, to develop an honest, intimate relationship.

To family and friends, their marriage appeared to be one of the best. As the wedding anniversaries came and went, family and friends commented on their loving thoughtfulness of each other; why, each wanted the other's opinion on everything! But when the company went home, George was a little boy again and his wife was the unwilling parent.

Their marriage had begun to deteriorate almost as soon as it was consummated. When George's bride recognized his inability to make and carry out a decision, she began to wonder what the future would be like. If she asked, "George, since we're going out for dinner, where would you like to go?" he would respond, "I don't know. Where would *you* like to go?" If she pressured him any more, he would say, "Go by yourself. There's food in the fridge, so I'm staying home." Gradually her opinion of him lowered to meet his own. George saw trouble coming, but he was not ready to admit that it was even partially his fault. He figured that women were flighty, irrational, over-emotional creatures; that was what made them the weaker sex. It was no use reasoning with them. Then again, the possibility had crossed his mind that anything he said might more or less incriminate him, so he settled back to rest on the old adage, "the less said, the better." He was not about to hazard a change in his life-style or outlook.

George was emotionally wounded a long time ago. Unfortunately, his wife was placed in the role of therapist and guardian, an inappropriate and unwanted role for her to manage. No wonder George avoided disclosure. He had to try hard to convince himself that he was the head of his home and that he was managing it the way it ought to be. He could see his wife's perplexity. He knew that she blamed him for the wall between them. The first price that George paid for his fear was loss of spontaneity and personal integrity. The second, potential loss was his marriage. The wall that he had erected to protect himself now imprisoned them both.

Walls can be hideous obstacles. While ministering in Europe in the early sixties, I was given the opportunity to visit a small band of West Berliners whose faith was challenged every day. Through the help of an interpreter, I learned that several members of this congregation had been torn from contact with their families in the Eastern sector. The Berlin Wall had only been up for a few short years, but it had already caused irreparable damage. Its irregularly shaped and forboding presence jutted into the lives of those people, shattering what families the world over enjoy: sharing family intimacy, secrets, traditions and memories. All this...until the Wall.

Garishly strewn at the foot of the Wall were flowers memorializing those who had been killed in heroic attempts to gain freedom in the West. In the midst of that tragic setting, a dramatic scene was enacted early every morning. Parents, grandparents and children climbed onto platforms of rough-hewn and nailed boards, trying to waft love messages across the politically imposed divide. At first their shouts could be heard. But only for a while. And then it happened. The Wall was built higher and higher until it completely blocked the view, cutting families to shreds with its impersonal shadow.

Need sparked ingenuity. As the Wall towered, so did the rickety stands supporting Western relatives trying to catch a glimpse, a wave, something of those cut off from the democratic world. In retaliation, East German soldiers reinforced the Wall with concrete slabs, barbed wire and steel I-beams like alien arms akimbo. Stark reality of separation was punctuated by the still, somber streets of East Berlin. Communication degenerated into scarred memory. The Wall was too high, too thick, too long.

As a relationship wall develops a thicker, more substantial foundation and superstructure, climbing around or over it becomes increasingly difficult. The spouse who tries to see over it finds his rickety stand more and more precarious. As the wall goes higher, communication becomes that much more limited and treacherous. Walls like that need to come down.

Discovered by Love [2]

Stone by stone it was built.
We never noticed.
Rather, it was always there,
    not built at all.

There it was.
The double wall of our two selves.

Behind them lie wide stretches
    of childhood, virgin woodland,
        where each may run off alone, gladly.
Their height and strength are reinforced
    by our years of strict education,
        righteousness, stern prohibitions.
They conceal the lost labyrinths
    of our adolescent years,
        made complex and confused by fear.
The stiffness of our lonely young years
    is in them.

And each of us has decorated his wall
    with a fine facade:
    a perfectly acceptable look,
    of being what we're expected to be,
    a man, a woman.
From the first we've acted out
    an elaborate comedy,
    each living inside himself,
    his own prisoner.

Will we go on taking good care of our walls,
    both of us, until we end up
    as total strangers?
Or can we, each and together,
    somehow breach the walls,
    bring them tumbling down
So that we might surmount their mingled ruins,
    and find opened out before us

the luminous, fertile land of our true selves interpenetrated, made one?

You Can Bring Your Walls Down

"In their self-will they digged down a wall" (Genesis 49:6, *KJV*). Walls exist because we will them to exist. Emotional walls in a marriage come down only when we agree to raze them together.

A marriage counselor endeavors to assess his counselees' motivation to change—their attitudes, their life-styles, whatever. He asks himself, "Why are these two people here? Do they want their marriage badly enough to make the needed changes?" Given sufficient motivation, almost any marital problem can be resolved. But you have to *want* it to happen.

When a troubled couple cannot seem to make headway in their efforts to improve their marriage, it is usually because of some strong, distracting factor. Often that distraction is a third party who is weakening the commitment they need to heal their marriage. The distraction does not have to be an adulterous liaison; it could be an autocratic employer, demanding clients, an education, domineering in-laws, even children. The Apostle James tells us, "A double-minded man is unstable in all his ways" (James 1:8). You *cannot* be double-minded, half-committed, and expect your marriage to be successful.

You *can* make your marriage into an intimate, harmonious relationship, that is, providing your efforts are unified. Like a land developer who has purchased a farmer's acreage for residential development, you and your partner need to draw up a plat—a layout of your immediate plans, priorities, and goals—and intend to accomplish them in toto.

Some of the most despicable marital relationships are directed to counselors like nuclear submarines on red alert. The warning is clear: If one less-than-failsafe button is tapped by mistake, programmed missiles could blow everyone away.

Friends of such a couple, reluctantly drawn into the heat of the war, perhaps forced to take sides, finally though hesitantly suggest a truce, a time to recoup, time to talk. The counselor's office is neutral territory where they meet to see if either marriage partner will allow ground for negotiation. Bitterly, the couple admit that the damage they have inflicted on each other has ricocheted and hurt family and friends around them. Ashamed of their exposure, they can begin to see what their real problems and challenges are.

The walls of hopelessness can be torn down in steps toward positive, productive negotiation. I have seen couples—whose marriage wars have ravaged both sides of the family—comprehend something of the destruction they have caused and begin to mend broken relationships. I have wept with couples through their separateness and rejoiced with them over their renewed vitality and emerging intimate connection.

Just as a problem does not gain a foothold overnight, neither will a solid solution be found and put into effect immediately. But once two people recognize the destructiveness of their marital disharmony, they will have taken a crucial step toward reconciliation. The next step will be admission that both have contributed to the disharmony and consequently both must contribute to the solution.

CHAPTER FOUR

Time and Time Again

How Much Time Is Intimacy Worth?

Time required for intimacy can exceed all other demands. Waiting for a lover is frustrating, especially when the moment for intimacy seems so right. Scheduled appointments, children's demands and even home-maintenance responsibilities can hinder moments of closeness that might have become treasured memories.

Betty had the table set. Every detail had been attended to. She knew what Bob liked. His taste for translucent china, imported lead crystal and formal dinnerware was evident because on his trips abroad, he always purchased something memorable for her, something that revealed his personal preferences as well as her own. The candles were lit, glowing with a warmth that radiated from Betty's smiling face.

Bob called. Dinner would have to be delayed for a few minutes. "I am hurrying," he said. "I can't wait to be with you."

Minutes turned into hours. The sliced apples in the Waldorf salad turned brown, the stuffed Cornish game hens on wild rice dried out, and the freshly baked dinner rolls turned into hardtack. Betty stared at her watch, paced back and forth in the kitchen, took a quick nap on the couch, glanced at the calendar to triple-check the date, then telephoned Bob's office.

His secretary, Leanne, answered. "Bob is working on the Lawson project. Looks like it's going to be a long night, Betty. Do you want me to give Bob a message for you?"

"No...I guess not. Thanks anyway, Leanne. 'Bye."

"Shut it all down," Betty thought to herself. "I give up. I've sure tried."

Going to the garage, she got into the car and headed for a fast-food restaurant to gorge herself with burgers and an Oreo milkshake. She pushed herself to take in a movie, something she had never done alone before, not ever. Her eyes would not focus clearly on the silver screen. All she could hear was Leanne's voice, "another long night." Betty thought of Bob's neglect, his always thinking of himself first when it came to his work and interests. She concluded that she must be the very last item on his priority list.

Back at the office, Bob is snowed with work. He feels imposed upon by his boss, his bills, even the distracting thought at the back of his mind that Betty is distressed and accusing. Pressure is building, and he would rather not go home at all now. Until he discovers that intimacy in his marriage relationship should be a priority second only to his commitment to God, he will always struggle over priorities. At some point a decision has to be made if simply because only so many things can be accomplished in the twenty-four hours of a day.

Marriage is the most important earthly relationship that we can have, and it must be cultivated. Far from last on the priority list, or even second, your mate has to be first. Unfortunately, Bob has already given Betty the impression that he is more concerned about his job than about her, and not once or twice, but consistently. The more he has said "no" when she suggested time together, the easier it has become for him to say. If it came to a showdown, he would choose Betty over his career. But his career is more insecure than his marriage, he thinks, so he must neglect her in favor of the career.

Intimacy—of necessity—takes time. Occasionally we hear the quip, "The *amount* of time you spend with your spouse is less important than the *quality*." In a recent survey, more than ninety percent of the couples who considered their marriage strong also said they spent a lot of time together. Conversely, divorced people usually said they had not spent much time with their "ex" before they split up.[3]

The Dry Rot Syndrome

A husband can easily take his wife for granted. After all, he sees her every day in familiar settings. The relationship can become habitual instead of exploratory. He is liable to lull himself into complacency by the comfortable, undemanding familiarity of his life-style until, one day, the doorbell rings.

Pretend you are Grant. You are still standing in the doorway, holding a divorce notice. This cannot be happening to you. It is ridiculous! You think of all the things you could have and should have done. You even begin to consider the hours of work on projects that took you away from your wife. At the time, that work seemed oh, so ultra-important. Why did you bother? Incredulously, you sift through the sheaf of legal documents that blank-stare back at you. A wave of panic almost stops your heart. You think of all the neglected hours you would like to repay your wife, hours that would represent the total investment of yourself. Now you believe you could give her that.

After a quick phone call to a friend who has been in a tight place himself, you dial a marriage counselor's number and make an appointment to see him. You reassure yourself that everything will be all right after you and your wife have talked things over. Only...how are you going to talk your wife into meeting the counselor with you?

Pulling yourself together, you tell her about the appointment; but your wife, expressionless and implacable, turns away without so much as a word. No retort could have been clearer or harsher. You are shocked by her lack of interest. What has gotten into her? Does she really want out of the marriage? Her determination is hard for you to understand.

What happened to you, in this scenario, is true of marriages affected by the dry rot syndrome. The veneer of the marriage—with the smiling faces and the insistence, "No problems here!"—was just fine, thank you. The inner structure was something else again; but from the outside, no one could see its neglect. In fact, most of the family and friends would be surprised to hear the news.

Dry rot is deceiving. On the surface, everything appears to be all right; but poke around on a plank that has dry rot and you will see what I mean. The plank has changed on the inside. What was once healthy, solid wood has turned into useless powder. Unfortunately, many marriages that look solid from the outside have dry rot inside.

Dry rot in a marriage comes from indifference. People and flowers grow in a warm climate. For your marriage to grow, you have to nurture your relationship with emotional warmth, with knowledge and with time together. You must *take* the time you need to establish intimacy, to reach out to each other and to communicate who you really are, in an atmosphere of loving, nonjudgmental acceptance. No one knows how much time you need to become intimate, but it definitely exceeds the length of time most people take to decide whether or not to marry.

You see, getting to know your mate intimately is a process that will continue throughout your marriage, not only in its first romantic phase. The knowledge and understanding that you need to sustain your marital commitment cannot come about through chance and fleeting encounters. Disciplined effort, with blocks of time set aside for that purpose, is the only way to establish and reinforce a strong and lasting relationship.

Intimacy Is More Than Friendship

The best kind of intimacy is "for better or for worse." No matter what the outcome of our sojourn in life, my wife's and my commitment to each other must tie us together...*always*. Should one of us become incapable of expressing love, the other must remain as a bastion of strength. That kind of commitment to a relationship is much more than that of friendship.

Friends base their connections upon common interests as well as personality characteristics, not upon romantic passion for each other. That is an important distinction, for when two friends become *passionate* for each other rather than for some other common interest, their relationship is developing into romantic love. The external interest has been replaced with their devoted interest in each other.

Now and then I hear couples say they have decided to go through divorce, parting amicably as good friends. They think they can take the sting out of the divorce decree.

Yes, your mate *should* be your best friend. There is no doubt about that. But to insist upon being good friends after divorce—at least from the rejected mate's point of view—is abusive. Divorcees may try to appear as though they have not been wronged or as though they do not feel guilty for leaving their former partner or children, and they may carry off that impression as far as others are concerned. Yet, someone who has experienced the passion, the emotional highs and physical joys of marital intimacy, can rarely settle for less after divorce...voluntarily. If one does, it is because no options seem available. Personal feelings are squelched in the family's best interest. Suppressing those feelings may be that person's way of avoiding unpleasant confrontations.

Intimacy Is More Than Communication

The problem with verbal communication is the possibility of misinterpretation. Expression is limited by language nuances and colloquialisms that get in the way instead of clarify. Limited vocabulary, lack of self-knowledge and filtered meanings by a listener make communication difficult. Because of those limitations, many people withhold their feelings and ideas. They think they have already been misunderstood enough.

As I sit at my word processor, I constantly search for better ways to express my thoughts. No words seem to project them fully and accurately. When I am hampered by a momentary inability to write, I take a break, hoping that some distraction will refresh my thoughts. The same tactic helps when there is a communication breakdown between two marriage partners, that is, unless communication is avoided altogether. Communication, you see, is a *requirement* for intimacy, but quality communication is a *result* of intimacy. As our facility at good communication grows, our intimacy grows. Communication and intimacy are interdependent. No couple can do without healthy communication.

Recognizing what enhances your relationship is essential to developing intimacy. That may mean carefully selecting the right words to say at the right time...or saying nothing at all. It has been quipped, with justice, "Often the difference between a successful marriage and a mediocre one consists of leaving about three or four things a day unsaid." Occasionally our responses would be insensitive even to the point of being callous, and those are the times we had better say nothing. An example of poor timing is when a husband walks into the kitchen while his wife is hurriedly preparing dinner, their toddler hanging onto her dress, a determined puppy pulling at her shoelaces, and preschoolers running about, and takes a notion to talk about sex. If he is wise, he won't. His lack of sensitivity would not only frustrate his wife, but create the impression that he does not consider her immediate needs important.

However, saying the right words the right way is not always necessary, either. Has anyone ever told you the story of the Polish immigrant and his South African bride? Conversation was difficult for them because neither knew much of the other's language. One day, after his wife had left to visit her relatives, the young man used an English dictionary to help put his thoughts down on paper. "Everywhere in home is a lack of you," he wrote, and mailed the note. She came home on the next train.

The immigrant's handle on English was not the best, but his "wrong" words had the desired effect. They told his wife that everything he saw reminded him of her and he missed her terribly. He had to tell her. What he wrote was just what she wanted to know.

Communication is *more* than the right words. It is an attitude, a willingness to reveal the secrets of your heart, your concerns, the love of your life. Those are the things that matter, not your eloquence. Do not hide behind a wall of apparent indifference because you are unsure of your ability to express yourself well. All communication takes is practice and a willing partner.

What is the unmentioned taboo in your communication? What is it that you refuse to talk about, that makes you walk on cat's feet when the subject is alluded to? What is the problem you have set aside because it is too volatile? Do you have a difference of opinion or sensitive topic that you hope will never come up? Of course you do. We all have areas that when touched raise our defenses. You know that those areas need to be addressed. You know intuitively that you must get them out into the open. How else can your mate know what is smoldering inside you? Unless your mate is tuned to your wave length, and vice versa, your attempts to reach each other will be unsuccessful.

The other element of good communication is simple. It is what most counselors learn in the early stages of their professional experience, and that is to *listen*. There are three rules for counseling that apply to marriage. The first rule is to *listen*. The second rule is to *listen*. The third rule (you guessed it) is to *listen*. By listening, you show respect for the person who is talking to you. You let your mate know that you value what you are hearing. Eminent Swiss psychiatrist Paul Tournier wrote, "Some men complain of the poor health of their wives without realizing that the latter are sick simply because their husbands never listen to them."[4]

I am no longer surprised when a woman comes to the counseling center because, she says, it is the only place where she feels she will be listened to and taken seriously. The counselor becomes a significant person because he listens with concentration, something his counselee desperately desires from her husband but which, for a variety of reasons, he does not offer. A wall of silence has separated the couple and eventually turned into contempt. The antidote is to remove the wall, breaking it down brick by brick until both marriage partners can see over it, and then help them to understand that openness and intensified interest in each other will bring about the warm relationship they need.

Intimacy Is More Than Understanding

"If only I could understand her!" exclaims the exasperated husband. After years of study, Sigmund Freud still asked, "What is it that a woman wants?"

For centuries, men have complained of the impossibility of deciphering the needs and wants of their wives. Women, too, have puzzled over their husbands.

Almost anything can cause consternation, including housekeeping. Bob, who has worked all day with tidy columns of figures, structured every minute of his time to accomplish his tasks, nearly suffers a seizure when he walks into the house and sees a total mess. His wife, Susan, was housecleaning; but somehow the more she cleaned, the more insurmountable the mess became until she collapsed, exhausted, on the sofa. Company will be ringing the doorbell in an hour.

Emergency sirens go off in Bob's head and he scrambles to put order into chaos. Tears run down his wife's cheeks and she sobs, "You think it's so simple. Well, it isn't!"

"It *could* be simple, but you aren't organized," Bob responds, exasperated.

Unwilling to let him do all the work, Susan ran to help. The housecleaning issue was brought up the following evening—after the house was straightened up, after the make-your-own-salad buffet was readied, after the company was gone (satisfied and happy, since Bob and Susan were excellent hosts), after the mess left in their wake was cleaned up, after Bob and Susan had had a night's rest. Only then did they discuss The Terrible Day the Company Came.

In their situation, Bob and Susan need to work out the housekeeping system together, pooling their creative and organizational skills. The key to accomplishing that teamwork is *empathy*. Bob and Susan could have argued and never come close to the cause of the problem, expressing only their own hurt feelings. Neither would have been particularly wrong, what each of them said would have had some merit. Fortunately, however, they waited until they cooled down and had time to attempt a meaningful understanding. Now they have the opportunity to do something positive that will benefit them both.

Your attentive listening and compassionate attitude will show your mate that you care. Of course, the attention and the listening that lead to empathy and understanding are costly. You will find that the result is worth the cost.

Not long ago, a very self-confident man was seated before me. He was a respected professor, he had many friends, and he was good at taking charge in difficult situations, but he needed help with his faltering marriage. In explaining his relationship with his wife, he said, "I include my wife in everything. I discuss everything with her." He went on to tell me of his personal interests, not once mentioning his wife's concerns. When I asked him what she thought about the things we had discussed, he replied, "She would never understand. I don't raise those issues at home." He admitted that he thought she would not agree with him and he did not want to argue with her. Those issues were crucial to the success or failure of their marriage, yet he was avoiding the potential for mutual understanding and agreement.

Having unloaded a few problems of my own on family and friends over the years, I can attest to the incredible relief in talking to an empathetic friend, to be heard, to be respected, to be comforted, to wrestle with issues and find helpful, new ideas. The moment of heart harmony with another, the moment of understanding, is a lofty experience something like the process of forgiveness Christ offers us: "Cast all your anxiety upon him because he cares for you" (I Peter 5:7).

Intimacy Is More Than Acceptance
"Bill's wife always laughs at his jokes. They must be pretty clever," a neighbor said admiringly. "No," his wife responded, "but *she* is!"

Some behaviors, such as that of the storyteller who spiels off endless strings of jokes (some of them vintage, others with a vague punchline, some too fishy to be swallowed, and some dandies, too) every time he can collar a listener, are due to the desire for acceptance. The practical joker and the gambler also try to make it big with an audience. But if we try to impress our mate that way, we are liable to be disappointed.

Acceptance in marriage, approval of ourselves and each other, takes more than a peaked hat and bulbous red nose. Acceptance requires trust, taking the risk to be ourselves. If you are unsure of whether or not your mate accepts you as you are, you need to ask yourself if *you* accept yourself the way you are. And to accept yourself, you need to allow Christ to demonstrate His genuine acceptance and help you.

"As the Father has loved me [Jesus], so have I loved you. Now remain in my love. If you obey my commands, you will remain in my love, just as I have obeyed my Father's commands and remain in his love"

(John 15:9,10). By dealing with spiritual acceptance first, you are addressing the ultimate values of mankind. Nothing supercedes these values; they are life-enhancing or threatening, depending upon your decision to accept or reject the claims of Christ. Then you will be able to work on the personal habits that have developed because of your neglect of spiritual values.

Requiring your mate to accept you before you can accept yourself is presumptuous. The psalmist asks God, "Keep back thy servant also from *presumptuous* sins; let them not have dominion over me" (Psalm 19:13, *KJV*). Allow God to complete the work of acceptance.

Intimacy Is More Than Sex

Some people think that sex is the greatest wound mender and communication enhancer around. No wonder, then, that when the mechanics of sex prove unsatisfactory, sex's problem-solving value vanishes, too.

Although a great experience, sex is not a panacea. If it were intended to be the goal of an intimate relationship, it would not be subject to whim and fancy. Sex is a symbol, *the product of* an intimate relationship already operative and productive. Of itself, it cannot stabilize a rocky marriage relationship.

Intimacy is more than friendship, more than communication, understanding, acceptance and sex. Intimacy includes all of that and much, much more.

PART TWO
Turn Your Potential Into Reality
(The How-To's)

CHAPTER FIVE

Nine Seasonings to Savor

Loving Is an Affair Every Day, Not Everyday Fare

A healthy, intimate relationship develops through careful, daily attention to nine seasonings, each beginning with the letter *c*: *counsel, confidence, companionship, confrontation, consistency, caring, commitment, conversation* and *contract*. Whichever combination of seasonings you and your mate choose to emphasize reflects your uniqueness. As with snowflakes, stars and innumerable other creations in the universe, no two couples are alike. Try to determine your level of intimacy by weighing your experience against the nine seasonings of an intimate relationship. Then think of improvements to work on...or even to make the initial effort. Watch for questions; and when you come to them, discuss them with your mate. By going through this chapter slowly and carefully, you will do more, *far more,* than deepen your philosophical understanding of intimacy, that is, if you read with the full intention of putting it into practice.

Ask Your Mate for *Counsel*

No special training is required for someone to be a *counselor,* in the general sense of the term. When making travel arrangements for a recent speaking engagement, a receptionist said that a counselor would be with me shortly. You can receive counsel about clothing, life insurance, real estate, weight loss, computer software and a million other things. It is in this general sense—in an all-inclusive, helping relationship—that you and your mate are your own counselors. From listening to doing (recognizing the impossibility of remaining completely unbiased or objective in your viewpoint), you are counseling each other.

Who do you talk to *first* when you are looking for new ideas, advice or encouragement? Do you call your pastor? A friend? Or, do you call your mate? Do you trust your mate enough to ask hard questions, even the ones that evoke strong opinions?

When you want to purchase new carpeting for your living room, who do you consult? If you would like to go deer hunting on opening day, do you make the decision arbitrarily? Do you ask a hunting buddy what he thinks, or do you confer with your mate? Given an important decision, do you turn to the one who it will likely affect as much as you, or do you turn to someone else who you know will say "yes"?

Out of the book of Proverbs comes the line, "Perfume and incense bring joy to the heart, and the pleasantness of one's friend springs from his earnest counsel" (Proverbs 27:9). Important decisions require objectivity, as much of a grip on truth as you can muster. That opens your lines of reasoning to the possibility of variant levels of understanding and different conclusions. If you would rather have your own way, if you wrinkle your nose as though you detect the essence of skunk whenever your mate hazards an opinion, you limit your perspective and harm your relationship.

By denying your mate's right to vote, you say in effect, "I am in control of you and me and everyone else I can manipulate or exploit." Any attitude that is not generous, that is not sharing, is also not conducive to intimacy. By giving your mate the right to vote, to say "aye," "nay," or whatever, you say, "You are important to me, and I respect your reasoning and feelings. I trust you to respond in a way that benefits both of us."

Respectful consideration should be due neither to fear nor to awe, but to your ability to accept your mate's reasoning in light of his or her vantage. Sometimes you know why your mate reacts in a particular way, and you take that into objective consideration, too. Serious, consistent consideration of your mate's opinions will nurture your relationship, and the roots of intimacy will grow deeper.

Do you take your mate's ideas and concerns seriously? If you ask your mate for an opinion, are you convinced that his or her reasoning is sound enough to put into effect? If not, why not? When you receive ideas and conclusions that differ from your own, do you sulk, respond angrily, do what you want to anyway? Or, do you graciously consider the counter viewpoint as a viable way to look at the situation? Does it make you feel good to have been included in the decision-making process?

Keep Confidences

"She told me that you told her the secret I told you not to tell her," Mrs. Hattie Green huffed. "Why, the mean thing! I told her not to tell you I told her," replied Mrs. Lucy Red, her next-door neighbor, who was just as indignant. "Well, Lucy," said Hattie, "don't tell her that I told you she told me!"

"Can you keep a secret, sweetheart?" asked Larry's wife. "Of course I can, hon, but it's just my luck to tell things to guys at the office who can't!"

"Are you sure we aren't gossiping?" asked Mary. "Of course not!" her sister replied. "This is just family chatter."

Broken confidences can ruin relationships, careers and futures. A young psychologist I once knew made a serious blunder while on the staff of an East Coast church. The referring pastor suspected that a counselee he had referred to the psychologist was homosexual, and because the counselee held a prominent position in his church, wanted a psychologist's opinion. Unfortunately, the psychologist said, "Yes, I think she *is*." He regretted his words as soon as he said them, but the damage was done.

Whether or not he had confidence in the pastor's discretion, the psychologist had not received a signed release from his counselee to discuss the circumstances with anyone. Attempting to stave off more trouble, he extracted a promise from the pastor not to reveal what he had said to anyone else. In spite of that precaution, the pastor broke his promise almost immediately, and within a matter of days, the counselee phoned the church office, threatening legal action for slander.

What could happen? Neither the psychologist nor the pastor knew how serious the repercussions would be, but they were uneasy for awhile. Not only did the psychologist fear for his ministry and practice, but he realized the agony his counselee was going through. Fortunately, the matter did not go as far as litigation. Yet, who would go to him for counseling if they knew that he had broken a confidence? That was a hard lesson to learn, but he learned it. And there you have the point. If you are unable to keep a confidence, your friends and business associates will soon find out and avoid sharing their concerns with you. More important, your mate may close his or her heart to you.

Telling secrets is a tantalizing temptation, especially for those who feel one-up if they have startling news, scandalous information that no one else has been able to get their hands on, as though they hold the first rights to a hot, legitimate news item! A photograph would be almost better, real *proof*. How talebearers love the Watergates and Irangates of life, that is, as long as they are on the investigative side of issues. They become authorities. They may even wield manipulative, blackmailing power because they know the truth, at least truth as they conceive it to be.

In troubled marriages, it is generally the case that one or the other partner struggles with personal disclosure. The reason is simple: He or she has been betrayed before. When a breach of confidence is discovered, the marriage relationship is damaged, to what degree depending upon the circumstances. The one who has been hurt may heap disabling guilt upon his or her partner, causing even more damage.

Keep confidences. You will honor your mate and strengthen your intimate relationship. I am fortunate to have a wife whose mouth is sealed about the feelings, hurts and joys I have shared with her. In twenty years of marriage, I cannot remember a moment when Margaret lapsed in her integrity. When she says something about me, she says something good. She is my most trusted friend and confidante. Yes, there have been times when she and I have disagreed with each other, but our disagreements are ours alone. Margaret has given me an important gift: *confidentiality.* Good marriages are confidential.

Can you always keep a secret? Perhaps you have one secret that you have kept from your mate. If so, what is it? Does it make you feel important to discuss what another person has told you in confidence? Are you willing to listen to your mate with a non-judgmental attitude? Can you tell your mate something with the confidence that it will never reach another person's ears without your permission? If not, have you shared your misgivings with your mate?

Be Your Mate's Closest *Companion*

Abraham Lincoln said, "The best way to defeat an enemy is to make him your friend." If you and your mate have suffered your own civil war, or if you have narrowly missed declaration of war, how can you establish a peace accord? Keep that thought in mind as we consider the third characteristic of intimacy: *companionship.*

After years of addressing congregations during Sunday morning worship services, I have developed the habit of perusing my sermon notes over early morning breakfast at a local restaurant. Now and then, my attention will be drawn to a couple who have lazily accommodated themselves to a welcome day off by having breakfast served to them. Fractions of a minute after they place their order, the husband flashes out the newspaper and begins to read. His wife cannot talk to him because his attention is at an Associated Press or United Press location.

Unless she has a section of the paper herself, all

she can do is look at the back of the paper he is holding or perhaps notice with a little start that I am glancing inconspicuously, I hope, at them. If she demands her husband's attention—"Charlie, I am *talking* to you"—he reluctantly lowers the paper and reaches for his coffee cup, nodding vacantly at her remarks until another opening comes for him to return to world, national and local gossip printed authoritatively in black and white. Do you think companionship can thrive that way? I don't think so.

What do you talk about when you are alone with your mate? Do you do all the talking, or do you do the listening? Do you talk about the children, your job, your friends, maybe some gossip? Do you feel lonely, isolated, or on a different wave length altogether? Do superficialities dominate your dialogue—inane, uninspired topics like the barometer reading, hectic daily schedules, traffic congestion? Are your conversations built around external topics rather than feelings, desires, needs, hopes, fears and other personal issues? What have you made of your life together? Most people crave personal attention, yet so often settle for so little.

Picture this counseling situation. It happened. Fran was impatient. She could not keep from interrupting, so she seldom heard her husband finish a sentence. He had no opportunity. As a result, she complained, "Allen never talks to me. I have no idea what he is thinking about."

Their lack of communication led them to a counselor, who put a piece of tape over Fran's mouth, enabling her to hear what her husband desperately wanted and needed to say. Fran was irritated because of the tape, but little by little she realized that she could only feel close to Allen if she listened to him. If she did not listen, she could not hear him tell her he loved her. She could not enter his world without listening to him. Even if what Allen said was not entirely complimentary at that point, he was including her in his thoughts and in his future. Both Fran and Allen were encouraged that day.

The risen Christ is our best model of an empathetic companion. When with Him, we feel like Number One. He lets us know that we are important to Him, that we are included in His plans. Marriage should reflect the same kind of companionship. Accepting each other with our gestures, words and attitudes gives each of us the sense of security and value we need as well as lovely hopes. The warm and embracing gestures, the words *you* and *us* used often in our conversations, the attitudes of faith and trust, all these build the strength, joy and peace of a godly, sincere companionship. The companionship of brothers is strong, especially between those who have grown up together, weathered the stresses and learned to admire each other's individuality and successes. Yet the Scriptures tell us that we can become friends that stick even closer than a brother (Proverbs 18:24).

Who is your best friend? If not your mate, why not? Do you think it is possible to be married to your best friend? If you think you *are* married to your best friend, have you told your mate that? If you do not consider your mate your best friend, can you give viable reasons why not? What do you think it would take for someone to be your best friend? Think about those questions and come to some sort of conclusion about them. Then discuss your thoughts and feelings about them with your mate.

Confront Your Mate

"Better is open rebuke than hidden love" (Proverbs 27:5) is an old Hebrew saying that holds as much truth now as when it was written in the days of the Old Testament kings. What do you think? Do you agree or disagree that being rebuked is better than being ignored? Is there anything much worse than being treated as a nonperson without the privilege to have and to express opinions?

Most of us try to avoid confrontations, and a common technique is the cold shoulder. A man told me his wife had given him the cold shoulder for so long that he decided to get her a thermal shawl. The one who has made us angry also makes us uncomfortable. Although we do not want to show our anger in other unacceptable ways, we often repress our feelings and ignore the offender. It is possible for some to feel an incredible urge to deny the person's existence, and the way to do that is to refuse that person his or her right to an opinion.

Here are a couple of questions and suggested answers: *Question One:* What does a person subtly or not-too-subtly express by ignoring someone? *Answer:* He communicates that no matter what happens to the person he is ignoring, it does not matter to him. *Question Two:* What advantage does he get from ignoring someone? *Answer:* Very little. He deludes himself into thinking that he has eliminated the ignored person's influence upon him. It would be better to express openly and responsibly what he feels instead of gunnysacking his feelings and denying the ignored person the right to an opinion contrary to his own.

King Solomon offered this wisdom: "As iron sharpens iron, so one man sharpens another" (Proverbs 27:17). What do you think he meant? By stating your negative feelings clearly and with self-control, you show respect and sharpen your relationship with another person.

Now put that thought into this perspective: How will being up front with your partner sharpen your relationship? I suggest that it will show respect. You say indirectly, "You are important to me, and I am convinced that you are capable of handling my confrontation without allowing our relationship to be adversely affected. Otherwise I would not tell you exactly how I feel." Openness will do something else for you. Now the two of you can, at the very least, begin to talk about issues that were closed before. Whether you confront or are confronted, it will do you good to show the respect you both deserve by listening intently.

If you intend to confront your mate, keep Galatians 6:1,2 in mind: "Brothers, if someone is caught in a sin, you who are spiritual should restore him gently. But watch yourself, or you also may be tempted. Carry each other's burdens, and in this way you will fulfill the law of Christ."

A confrontation can take an unusual turn, too. A husband home from work angrily complains, "What! Isn't dinner ready? That's it. I'm going to a restaurant." His wife replies, "Wait just five minutes." "Why? Will it be ready by then?" he asks. "No," says his wife, "but then I will go with you."

When you confront your partner, is your confrontation precipitated by a crisis that blows you out of control? Or, do you confront responsibly when a problem arises? Does confrontation in your marriage always result in a retaliatory battle? Can you confront without raising your voice, blood pressure or fist? Does your mate see love in your confrontation, or do you have to give assurances that you acted out of love? If so, why?

Be *Consistent*

According to an old English proverb, "In time of prosperity, friends will be plenty; in time of adversity, not one in twenty." Is that because most of us are so success-oriented that if a friend begins to slide toward apparent failure, we fear that by associating with him we will fail as well? The distorted thinking that may cause us to believe that can also cause us to believe the opposite. We can delude ourselves into thinking that if one relationship becomes tangled, we can try another relationship, as if by sheer magic we can eliminate present difficulties.

Consistency builds character. Or, is it the other way around? Character builds consistency. I believe the latter is more true. If you find yourself unable to remain consistent in your attitude and responses to your mate, or if you are unfaithful to your commitment time and time again, you had better think about what it means to be a person of character.

Several years ago, while listening to the *Hour of Decision* radio broadcast, I heard Dr. Billy Graham talk about his personal relationship with God. Often, upon retiring for the day, the great evangelist stared through the darkness toward the ceiling as if peering into the searching eyes of God. He said the greatest feeling was to know that as far as he knew, absolutely nothing hindered his relationship with God, there was nothing between them that would make him wish he could hide from the penetrating eyes of his Creator. Dr. Graham did not mean that he considered himself perfect. Every one of us, no matter who we are, comes "short of the glory of God." He meant that he was forgiven for his sins and that he made a concerted effort to remain consistent in God's eyes. On those days when consistency seemed to have been reached, he felt a sense of wholeness and closeness with God.

Consistency, which in the sense I have used it here is really another word for *integrity*, seems to encourage consistency in others. If we are honest and truthful in our relationships, we give people the opportunity to trust us and allow them the freedom to be honest and truthful in return. Filibustering and groveling because of inconsistent behavior have never been accorded honor. Consistency, integrity, honesty and truthfulness build a marriage relationship. Inconsistency and hypocrisy break it down.

Are you dependable? Can your mate trust you

to be there when the going gets rough? Can your mate count on you for love and financial support? Do any distractions deter you from total involvement with your marriage? Does anyone question your ability to be consistent? Why? Are you willing to make any changes to alter that impression?

Care

Do you care about your companion? Do you care enough to communicate, to confront, to work out differences as they come up? Do you take care to note and attempt to meet your partner's needs? What does caring mean to you?

Fred and Jeanette asked me for help. Fred was carrying on an illicit liaison with another woman, and Jeanette had discovered it and bravely confronted him about it. He did not deny what was going on, nor did he seem to care what she thought. He expected Jeanette to accept his love affair with the other woman without any radical changes in their own personal relationship, a position that Jeanette refused to take. Fred was torn between two loves, wanting to keep them both without harming either. Jeanette felt betrayed.

Neither Fred nor Jeanette would back down, and only a crisis forced Fred to choose between the two. A summer weekend, while waterskiing, Jeanette became tangled in the ski ropes underneath their speedboat. Fred saw that she was in trouble and considered letting her drown (no one would have been the wiser). Jeanette's frantic motions finally brought out his sympathy, and he rescued her.

Fred had lost most of his reasons to care for Jeanette. What began as a one-time tryst, just a minor investment in another woman, clouded his perspective and directed his attention away from his wife and their future together. Personal challenges at work, in sports or hobbies can be less dramatic but just as threatening if they diminish your investment in your marriage. You see, caring is an investment that takes time and energy.

Do you care only when your mate is hurt, facing surgery, or laid off from work? Little things count. Do you care enough to do the little things to show you care...like picking up after yourself, walking the dog, twisting the cap tightly on the tube of toothpaste and returning it to the cabinet, shutting the garage door? Do you still say "You look nice today" and "I enjoy our talks together, just the two of us"? Do you remember to say "Thank you" with the same meaning that it carried when you were first married? Those may seem like inconsequential acts of thoughtfulness, but if the little things are neglected, the impression of carelessness can become a formidable barrier to good marriage management and a caring relationship.

In the course of marriage counseling, women frequently allude to low self-esteem because they believe that their husbands do not care about them. One young man abandoned his wife and daughter ostensibly because his wife's cooking and housekeeping compared unfavorably with his mother's. Within a few weeks he was married again, this time to a divorcee with children of her own. Now his mother has two sets of grandchildren and a heart almost as broken as his first wife's, but he shows as little care for his mother as he did for his first wife. Another man judges his wife's value by the amount of money she contributes to the family income, and another to the time she devotes to furthering their children's education by correcting their homework, gathering research materials and drilling them on their spelling and arithmetic lessons. Other than as live-in help, their husbands seem to care very little about them.

A bride who hears her groom proudly state his love and commitment to her "above all others" at the marriage altar may soon learn that she does not quite measure up to his expectations and for that reason does not deserve his care. A groom who has spent years in graduate school to earn a coveted degree and graduates only to find closed doors in his chosen field may be disheartened by his wife's decision to look elsewhere for someone to provide her with a more luxurious life-style. She doesn't care.

*Care*ful attention will usually elicit reciprocation in kind. *Care*ful awareness will deepen and broaden the love of two people, will develop strength and flexibility. When someone genuinely cares for me, I feel wanted and needed. I feel important to that person. You want to feel important to your mate, don't you?

When you show you care, why do you do it? Is it because you feel obligated to your marriage contract or because you sincerely care about your marriage partner?

Can you anticipate potential problem situations

that could make your mate despair? What can you do to help each other before a supposed or real calamity happens? Whatever you can do to prepare yourself for trouble will help. Begin to think about potential hazards now and down the road in your relationship. What can you do now that will help you then? Prepare for your future.

When you need personal attention yourself, can you comfortably approach your mate for that? Do you know that the response will be from a caring heart?

Commit Yourself

New romantic relationships possess an intensity of emotion and pleasure that is never forgotten. The discovery process between two lovers becomes intermittent over the course of a long marital relationship. Newness can tempt a partner to look beyond the bounds of marriage for the rejuvenating refreshment he or she remembers, and chances of being found out can lend an atmosphere of adventure similar to that experienced in adolescent dating.

Newness is the fountain of youth, the magic elixir, actually the mirage for which a person can sacrifice legitimate growing intimacy. The immediate, head-swimming gratification becomes more important than lifetime commitment, a family and a reputation. Even when faced with an ultimatum, pride and the obsession for newness will generally dictate the decision to abandon the past.

The abandoned mate becomes two-dimensional, a shadow rather than a person. It is true, is it not, that "familiarity breeds contempt," especially in a static, uncaring, *uncommitted* relationship. Marriage problems can be transferred entirely to the abandoned partner. What the adulterous mate wants is unavailable: a fantasy world unrelated to the necessary routines of romantic maintenance. Sadly, most learn that only after losing their mates, children and even their jobs.

Can you exhibit the kind of commitment that will break the odds against divorce? The statistics vary, but the margin is slim: One out of every two or one out of every three marriages in America will end in divorce. How can you prevent that from happening to yours? If your marriage is going to work, is it because you and your mate have such charming and irresistible personalities that nothing could turn you from your commitment to each other?

If you are going to honor your marital vows, if you are going to care for each other until the day you die, it will not be because of personality, manners, luck or pluck. It will be because of your straight-out commitment. Your grit and firm hold on God's hand will hold you together. Do not give up now. The only way to achieve togetherness is by the kind of commitment that nothing short of death can extinguish.

To be single again, oh, how glorious! All the burdens of life are gone! Is that true? Divorce will create a misery that you have never experienced before. Marital commitment means hard work, but *two* brows will sweat, not one.

Covenanted promises—made in the presence

of God and other witnesses—become increasingly important to those whose marriages have been tested in the crucible of His refining fire (see Malachi 3:2). As sure as they are married, couples will face trials and stresses that will take their best faith, wit and strength to withstand. Troubles come. They are inevitable. But just as a bone becomes stronger at the point of a break, their marriages will become stronger at each stress point. Commitment is the sure-fire stuff that substantiates one's romantic desire to make a marriage work against all the odds. Commitment means giving and giving and giving until it hurts. Commitment means never giving in, never giving up.

What does commitment mean to the two of you? Are you sure that your commitment goes beyond convenience? If you wrote out a promise to fulfill your marriage commitment to each other, would you tack on a list of if's and but's, perhaps some contingencies concerning money, physical beauty or job location? Do you have unwritten and unspoken stipulations to your commitment? Are there possible instances in which your commitment guarantee would be voided? Is your commitment based on the same biblical or philosophical foundations? Do you agree with each other about the ways in which you demonstrate your commitment? If not, can you think of ways to substantiate your vow convincingly?

Watch Your *Conversation*

Water from one well will not taste the same, nor

will it be of the same clarity as other well water. Water from a single well cannot taste salty and sweet, clean and contaminated at the same time. No matter how you test the water, the source always determines the result.

If you tell your mate, "I'm going to work all day Saturday, so don't plan on our ride along the North Shore," then go to the ballgame with the guys, there is an element of incongruity to what you have said. If you say, "I would love to have lunch with you, honey, but I have a load of laundry in the washing machine and one in the drier," then go out for lunch with a neighbor, what you have said does not seem to mesh with what you meant. If you say, "You are the most lame-brained male I have ever met!" or, "You are the dumbest blonde this side of the equator!" you will have a hard time adding, "But I love you."

James, traditionally identified as the Lord's brother, had this to say: "Out of the same mouth come praise and cursing. My brothers, this should not be. Can both fresh water and salt water flow from the same spring? My brothers, can a fig tree bear olives, or a grapevine bear figs? Neither can a salt spring produce fresh water. Who is wise and understanding among you? Let him show it by his good life, by deeds done in the humility that comes from wisdom" (James 3:10-13).

We need to say what we mean. Have you heard this? "It wasn't *what* you said, it was *how* you said it that told me you didn't mean a word of it!" Have you heard these lines? "Aw, I was just joking!" and

"Can't you take a hint?" What happens when crying "Wolf!" finally gets the response, "Is that right? Well, that is too bad because from past experience, I cannot believe you." The result is distrust and despair. The cure? *Begin* to speak the truth and *continue* to speak the truth. "Therefore each of you must put off falsehood and speak truthfully to his neighbor, for we are members of one body" (Ephesians 4:25).

True conversation communicates mutual high regard and inclusion in discovery and satisfaction. Do you converse with your mate? Do you converse truthfully? Do you believe what your mate tells you? Do you like to talk together? Do you include encouragement, supportive remarks, loving assurances, in your conversation? Do you show respect by the kind of language you use? Your mate is important to you. Show that in your conversation.

Honor Your *Contract*

Did you know what your mate's expectations would be of you when you were first married? Do you know what your mate's expectations are now? Have the expectations changed at all? Expectations can be vague, confusing, shifting. They can also be hard-and-fast rules. They can be reasonable or unreasonable. Expectations regarding roles, duties and responsibilities in marriage can express mutual respect or impertinence. They can be uplifting or denigrating. They can apply equally to each or be lorded over one.

Couples need to know what the expectations are, preferably before tying the wedding knot. More often than not, expectations are assumed on the basis of individual backgrounds and personal opinions. Gradually expectations become obvious, sometimes not so gradually. They may be a shock. Ideally each marriage partner will take care of his or her own responsibilities without a reminder. When one has evaluated and accepted responsibilities in order to fulfill marital obligations, it is his or her personal duty to see that they are carried out.

Contracts are made to be honored, especially marital contracts. What are the responsibilities of marriage? Discuss them with your mate. Do you see those responsibilities the same way you did when you were first married? How will you handle them now? Look at the biblical directions for husbands and wives in Ephesians 5:21-33 and Colossians 3:18,19. Do you agree on an interpretation of these verses? In practice? Are you fulfilling your roles as determined by your exegetical work on these passages, or are you only assuming that your roles are scripturally correct? Have you agreed upon your roles? Do they align with your interpretation of Scripture? If not, why not?

Intimacy is not to be found in frilly, heart-shaped boxes displayed in store windows on Valentine's Day. You will not find it in books. Intimacy is not a matter of words, either. How can you show your wife that you love her as Christ loves His bride, the Church? How can you show your husband that after Jesus, he comes first in your life? How can you cherish each other as the Scriptures outline for you in Ephesians 5:21-33 and Colossians 3:12-19?

Intimacy is a closeness that grows in proportion to the investment you put into it. If you are starting out in marriage, if you are experiencing some difficulty in marriage, or if you have as close to a perfect marriage as you can imagine, I encourage you to practice the nine seasonings of intimacy expressed in this chapter. If you are a child of God, He is transforming each of you more and more into His likeness, and your marriage will be transformed more and more into the kind of relationship He desires to have with His Church. Explore the possibilities.

Communication
Collision or Consensus?

Strewn across the floor were pieces of Jim's letter, a letter he had painstakingly crafted to explain his impetuous behavior the day before. He knew that he had blown it, and his wife, Darlene, had run to the garage before he could say anything more. The car engine had roared defiantly, the gear shift scraped into reverse, and the tires screamed.

Jim's mind painstakingly replayed what he had said and the explosive response he had witnessed. He was as bewildered as Darlene. After counseling with their pastor, they had honestly tried to communicate better by setting aside ample time, hours of time, to talk. Now, standing motionless at the kitchen counter, Jim thought about those long, intense hours of "communication" and concluded that the effort he and Darlene had put into it was a waste of time.

After racing down the country road, Darlene calmed down somewhat and turned in at a roadside cafe, hoping to find some consolation in coffee and quiet. She and Jim had stopped here for coffee many times. Ordering a cup "from the fresh pot," she gloomily thought of the dreams she had once had for their marriage, the romantic fireside chats at teen camp and the pre-marital counseling with their pastor. Somehow the aroma was not as rich as she had remembered, and the black brew was not soothing to her frayed feelings and jumpy nerves, but it warmed her throat, and she appreciated that.

Their marriage was blessed by both sets of parents, their pastor and their friends. Jim and she were Christians. They attended the same church. They were getting along all right financially, and there did not seem to be any particular problems except that they seemed to say the wrong things and assume the worst of each other. Darlene was puzzled and even a little frightened. Why didn't Jim understand her, and why was it so hard to understand him?

Like Jim and Darlene, many couples think that they have done everything possible to communicate. They have attended seminars, taken compatibility tests, followed pastoral counsel, read all the advice columns in the newspaper, checked out marriage counselors and tried to apply scriptural principles. If words alone could save their marriages, they would have been secure long ago. But words alone do not suffice.

Have you ever tried to reason with someone who was just pretending interest? Have you ever tried your best to express clearly, briefly and interestingly a topic of special importance to you only to realize that the best response you are getting is a glazed look and a yawn? You know that in another minute, your "victim's" eyelids will droop and he'll fall into a complete stupor.

What is the problem? The commitment to participate is weak or lacking altogether. The talk is all on one side. In that case, taking turns to talk does not make a difference, either. What does make a difference is mutual listening and responding with the determination to understand and be understood... and one more thing: the desire to make your marriage a happy one. Communication is more than words.

The wife who stares at her closet packed tight with clothes and says, "I haven't a thing to wear," does not really mean that. What she may actually mean is "Honey, I want something new and fashionable for the party tonight. I need it. I need something to make me feel really good about myself when I am with that self-assured, cosmopolitan group of people." Communication like that requires close attention and quick deciphering. Hopefully her husband knows at least three details: what the people are like, how she feels about them and how she feels about herself. There is also something just a bit unfair about this kind of communication in that it requires a sleuth's astuteness on the part of the listening partner and almost, but not quite, absolves the speaker from any guilt for stating (at this point only intimating), "I think I'll just go down to Neiman Marcus and spend $500."

How much do you dare to assume when your partner communicates indirectly? She might be thinking, "If he loves me, he will understand that I need to get a new dress. He will be so proud of me tonight! In another minute he will say, 'Dear, here is the checkbook. Go get yourself something nice to wear tonight.'" She might be thinking along different lines, too, such as, "I suppose he would be upset if I bought a new dress, so I might as well make the best of a less-than-desirable situation." She might even be thinking, "Oh, I wish I could have a new dress, but he is careful not to overspend, and I don't want to overspend, either. I will have to make do unless he suggests I get something new." The more you know about your partner, the more likely you will know how to respond.

Marriage requires a special kind of communication. In order for two people to respond to each other in a way that is mutually satisfying, each must have an empathetic feeling for the other. To say, "If I were you—" is never adequate, because none of us can actually *be* another. A more helpful statement would be, "I don't feel the same way, but I am trying to understand why you feel the way you do."

Communication requires quality talking, but more than talking; quality listening, but more than listening. Communication also requires the ability to project one's own feelings accurately. Do not deny your resentments, hostilities, or your love. You could choose to ignore negative thoughts, or you could choose to be honest, and as a result, healthier and probably happier.

While "speaking the truth in love" (Ephesians 4:15), try to anticipate the way your mate will respond. To do that is the mark of a sensitive person; it is also the mark of a person with common sense. How will an expression of your true feelings affect your mate? Do you know? Try to put yourself in your partner's place. Attempt to see through his or her eyes. Feel what he or she would likely feel.

Jesus saw through our eyes and felt what we feel. Incarnated, He relinquished the powers of His heavenly position and identified with us. He empathized with us. He knew our frailties and temptations. He willingly humbled Himself and died a man's death for our sake (Philippians 2:4-8).

Give the gift of empathy to your mate. Be wise, however, in how you express your ideas. Be calm and clear. Do not threaten or alarm your partner with exaggerations, theatrics or histrionics. Be logical. Distortion of the truth, which happens in an irrational angry outburst, for example, does more than complicate the issue; it hinders open communication and fair negotiation.

Do your best not to be defensive even when the issues are threatening. Defensiveness is also a hindrance to open, objective communication. Whether the attack is right or wrong, you can learn something from it. This is your opportunity to see how your partner perceives your words and behavior. If he or she is correct, you will be all the better for listening. On the other hand, if the observations are grossly exaggerated and radically differ from your own, you will gain valuable insight into why an impediment exists in your relationship. You will have additional facts and feelings to assist you in mending a distorted perception. Without this knowledge you would be no better off than you were before.

If you interrupt an attack and attempt to force your partner to see an issue the way you do, the discussion will escalate into a frenzied exercise in exerting control over each other. There will be more trouble ahead if that happens. So, turn your mate's criticism into an opportunity. By acknowledging the criticism, you show respect for his or her opinion. Acknowledgment does not require agreement, but registers your desire to show respect, making it possible to discuss ideas in a more neutral frame of mind.

Stick with the central problem. Avoid extraneous issues; they would dissipate the discussion's impact. Only after the primary issue has been resolved, or both of you have decided to file it away for discussion later, should you introduce another issue. By cooperating with each other to accomplish the resolution of issues one at a time, you will become better at empathizing.

Encourage empathy by finding a secure place for the two of you to talk. Be alone together. You might try a park or the beach. Depending upon how you feel and the issue at hand, you might even pick a favorite restaurant, but I suggest you go where you will have privacy. Pick a place both of you will enjoy. Clear, open and honest communication requires energy and concentration. Do not add frustrations by a setting that causes you to feel vulnerable or victimized. Get away from children, work and friends. Your marriage is far more important than short-term neglect of your routine responsibilities. Give yourselves a chance to communicate.

Oh, yes, there is something to remember: *Show respect*. Try to understand your mate's feelings and ideas instead of automatically rejecting them. If you adopt a positive attitude; if you decide to take the chance of being open and honest; if you want to make up for days, weeks, months or years of wasted time; if you want to see something good happen, *show respect*. You will increase your potential for good, sound, healthy communication. You will increase the potential for developing empathy. And in developing empathy, you will increase the potential for developing mutual respect, caring and love.

Do you know what an accepting climate is? It is a mutual agreement not to judge what is said on the basis of its correctness. To say, "I see that another way, but I am trying to understand your point of view" is nonjudgmental. To bellow, "You're crazy!" is judgmental. To be nonjudgmental is to honor and assist your partner.

Paul, who taught early church Christians how to live in harmony as members of God's family, wrote this: "Be devoted to one another in brotherly love. Honor one another above yourselves" (Romans 12:10). As Christians, we do not have the personal extravagance of selfishness. Not only is selfishness spiritually unhealthy, but it is also emotionally unhealthy. Selfishness is the enemy of all relationships, heavenly and earthly. It is the cause of wars, conflicts, personal battles. Selfishness is sin. No other problem takes precedence over this one. Selfishness causes every other problem. It is always ready to turn a Christlike attitude of love into a diabolical attitude of "Gimme! I want! Let me! I will!" and the inevitable "I hate you!" The cure for selfishness is only found in Christ.

God's Son modeled communication skills by His relationship with His Father and with the people around Him during His ministry on earth. Although our attempts at communication reflect His imperfectly, we can emulate the love, character and empathy that God has shown for us. That is our goal. God expects us to become persons of Christlike integrity, "to be conformed to the likeness of his Son" (Romans 8:29), and that includes our communication. Revealing and hearing the truth clearly communicated is a liberating experience. "You will know the truth, and the truth will set you free" (John 8:32).

Coming to agreement through communication includes discovering your differences. Being separate and unique persons trying to communicate means that differences will emerge and those differences can either improve or destroy your relationship. Being aware of differences is a priority for honest communication and closeness. Communication: collision or consensus? As we become more and more like Christ, communication leads to *consensus*.

Discovering Differences

A Not-So-Trivial Game

Do you think you *know* your mate? Are you sure? I will soon be asking you questions and giving you opportunity to interact with each other. The *Discovering Differences* game is a trivia game of sorts, but the little jigsaw pieces transform what might be a puzzle into a portrait.

The book of Genesis records the information that "Adam *knew* his wife; and she conceived" (Genesis 4:1, *KJV*). I remember reading that as a boy, and I could not help chuckling. I knew what that *knew* meant. I certainly thought I did.... If Adam and Eve were bold enough to have intercourse, why wasn't the Old Testament historian bold enough to come out and say so? At the same time, I wondered why the original Hebrew term was translated in such a way that it did not explain exactly what happened. That little word *know* caused all kinds of confusion to a young man who was unschooled but exceedingly curious about sex. I had a lot of questions.

What does *know* mean to you? Would you translate it with the word *sex*? Does *to know* equate with *sex*? Is sex the sum of knowing? Of course sexual knowledge, knowledge about someone's body, personality, gestures, does not constitute love. Of itself, knowledge has nothing to do with intimacy. Knowledge is the strongbox in your mind that contains what you consider to be facts.

Our concern with knowledge is how it applies to and encourages intimacy. Say two glances meet and hold across a crowded room, say two people find each other interesting when competing for an antique piece of furniture at an auction, say a handsome young man assists a lovely young woman onto her horse in a first English riding lesson. Would you say it was possible for two people to "fall in love at first sight"? There is very little evidence to show that could happen. They might fall into interest, fall into fantasy maybe, or decide to initiate a friendship; but ignorant, misleading, indiscriminate, immature feelings and intuitions are not the substance of love. First impressions can be wrong, oh, so wrong.

If you are going to fall in love with someone, you need to *know* something about that person. You need to put your reasoning power into action. Facts, figures, time and experience will weigh the potential for and eventually the strength of a relationship. Getting to know someone, learning to love someone, means dissolving misconceptions, melting mirages, creating a true picture insight by insight.

When a woman says, "My husband does not talk to me," I am led to believe that she is being denied the details, the feelings and the thoughts that would keep him clearly, fully in her mind. The less she knows, the more he goes ahead without her, the weaker the bond becomes between them. How do you keep a subject clear in your mind? By ignoring it? If, for example, you needed to learn and remember a series of commands in order to make good use of a computer spreadsheet program, would you pay attention to the instruction manual? Or would you ignore it and hope to know how to run the program without any information? You cannot successfully maintain, much less enrich, your marriage relationship without giving attention to your partner. Keep his attention, keep her attention by giving quality information, by honestly asking for opinions, by showing real concern, by complimenting and encouraging, by being helpful, by forgiving and loving.

When you take a chance at revealing a part of yourself, when you allow yourself to be vulnerable, you offer your partner the same opportunity. When you allow your partner to feel secure, you will—if indirectly—be helping yourself because how a partner behaves influences how his or her partner will react. A negative attitude almost automatically engenders a negative response. A positive attitude, with patience, should eventually create a positive response.

Think about this. If a small boy, from whatever foreign country, who knows only a smattering of gutter English, enters the American school system and is hurt by the taunts of uncaring, ignorant schoolmates, what will happen? He will become distrustful and bitter. How could you, if you were an elementary school counselor, win that child over? How could you change his hurt to health, distrust to trust and bitterness to appreciation? You would begin by recognizing the problem. Then you would attempt to learn as much as you could about the child's background and the children who were misusing him, probably by talking to teachers and parents.

Then what would you do? Considering all of the information you had, you would decide how to approach the little boy directly. Once you had made the first contact, you would try to see him casually as often as possible, always offering a word of encouragement and attempting to get as much response as you could. Patiently, gently, in time, you would win his confidence and develop a positive relationship. To help him, you would have to be genuine, with the sincere motivation to help. You would have to be knowledgeable, and you would have to take the time to give him the attention he needs.

Your marriage relationship is something like that of the unhappy little boy and the counselor who wants to be his friend. To receive attention, you must give attention. To be known, you must learn to know. To know, you must allow yourself to be known. To receive respect, you have to show respect. To be given time, you must give your time. To be secure, you must offer security. To be trusted, you need to trust. To trust, you must do everything you can to help your partner to be trustworthy. Do you see what I mean? To experience a gracious spirit, show grace. To experience generosity, be generous. How you behave will, to a large extent, determine how your partner will respond. Two positives make a positive. Two negatives make a negative. Potentially, one positive can transform a negative into a positive.

Take that potential and turn it into a probability. Now the question is how to do that. You already have a picture in your mind, whether vague or clear, of the ideal mate. If you are a Christian, elements of that picture may be derived from I Corinthians 13, the Apostle Paul's chapter on love. Read verses 4-8, substituting "love" for the older term, "charity":

> "[Love] suffereth long, and is kind; [love] envieth not; [love] vaunteth not itself, is not puffed up, doth not behave itself unseemly, seeketh not her own, is not easily provoked, thinketh no evil; rejoiceth not in iniquity, but rejoiceth in the truth; beareth all things believeth all things, hopeth all things, endureth all things. [Love] never faileth..." (*KJV*).

The loving husband and wife ideally exhibit those characteristics. Granted, as Christians we are to grow into the image of Christ. Not one of us has achieved His perfection, yet to do so is our common goal. As we look to Him for strength and wisdom to strive toward that goal, as we work on each characteristic, we will find ourselves relating better to our mates, to our children, to everyone we know.

Let us go back to the picture in your mind of the ideal mate. At this point, decide whether or not that picture is true to I Corinthians 13. Is it? Now, are there elements in that picture that come from Hollywood screen writers? How about tour ads? Is there just the hint of irresponsibility or escapism in the characteristics you see in the picture? Are there contradictions in that picture? Do you actually see two images: one that expresses your Christian beliefs and one that expresses a desire to do your own thing? How do you think those pictures affect your real-life relationship with your mate?

Can you ever be satisfied with your mate if the satisfaction you desire is related to an unrealistic or contradictory image of the ideal mate? That is something you need to think about. Undoubtedly your image of the ideal mate has changed and will continue to change as you grow older. It will be related to your faith in Christ, your endeavors to become more like Him and the influence of the media and people around you. That image is actually a reflection of what you would like for yourself. It is, to some lesser or greater extent, a reflection of you just as you are at this moment.

As you grow into the image of Christ, your conception of the ideal mate will also become more Christlike. The biblical model will become more and more important to you, for only as an individual grows into the image of the Creator will he or she experience wholeness and personal fulfillment. Once you have decided to live a Christ*like* life founded upon God's Word (specifically for now, upon I Corinthians 13:4-8), then you will have gained, among others, two major benefits: You will have a solid model for living (God's Word, the Bible), and you will begin to understand how important it is for you and your mate to work out the Christian life together. You need to help each other to develop a meaningful life on earth that leads inevitably to eternal life with your Creator in heaven.

In working together on this project, you have two learning objectives: to know each other and to know God's plan for you both. The first objective is accomplished by asking each other questions, the second by studying God's Word together. Ask questions as you read the Bible and look for the answers *in the Bible*.

Nothing can replace your Bible study and prayer together, nor should it, but you also need to focus on personal questions and answers apart from those times. Asking each other questions can be fun, sobering, inspirational or tender. Whatever, asking questions and empathizing with the answers will be enlightening. That is a primary way to get to know your mate and so a primary way to strengthen the bond between you. Do you know how to ask questions that require more than a *yes* or *no* response? Try these openers: "What happened when...?" and "Why...?" "Tell me about..." Quality questions and quality answers require quality thought.

There are three ways to learn through questions. First is the *story*. Be prepared to hear and to tell a detailed, true story. For example, using the story approach you could ask, "Do you remember your grandparents? What were they like?" and your partner could begin, "Oh, Grandpa died when I was two years old, and most of what I know about him I have heard from Mother. Grandma came to live with us..." and be off to a great start. "I remember when..." will help to take you back to an episode of your life and to relive it in memory. Express what happened just as it goes through your mind. Your partner will be caught up in the story with you. As the story unfolds, you and your partner may feel the emotions as you felt them then: the joy, the sorrow, the discovery. In a sense, you will be there together.

The single question, "What don't I know about you that I should?" is the second approach to learning through questions. Whether you ask each other this question daily or yearly, you will be amazed by what you learn. Whether a couple has been married for a month or fifty years, this simple question surfaces some of the most mundane and some of the most profound experiences. You might share a minor detail from your childhood, such as being just a little bit afraid when the state fair Ferris wheel stopped with you at the top. The chair swung gently back and forth. Miles and miles of air, it seemed, stretched between you and the ground. Shouts and laughter wafted louder and softer, depending upon the direction of the wind currents. And then the great old wheel jerked into life again, the chair wobbled, you clung to the safety bar in front of you and slowly descended to the platform. When you got off the chair, you made a mental note not to ride on one of those machines again.

When asked, "What don't I know about you that I should?" you might share what your partner's thoughtfulness in a certain situation meant to you. "Yesterday when you picked the rose, I watched you from the window. You smelled it and smiled. Then you brought it to me. Honey, that smile was worth more than all the roses on earth." You could answer with something entirely different, but always say something that will express something about yourself that you would like your partner to know.

You might express the feelings you had on your first day of school or a hurt you felt when you thought your best friend had rejected you. Those details may seem insignificant now, and probably are because you see them from an entirely different perspective, but they will add increasing traces of information to the bank of personal knowledge you have about your mate, giving you more reasons to love and more data to contemplate. The details will add substance to your feelings, so if you do not feel on top of the world, you will still have *reason* to love each other. Intimacy depends upon knowledge.

The third approach is the *Discovering Differences* game. Similar to the "What don't I know about you that I should?" exercise, this game will give you more and more in-depth insights to each other. This game may be somewhat more complicated because you may not know in how many ways your partner differs from you. Your goal is to learn what he or she is like and to express some of what you are like deep down inside.

What may seem to be a trifle cockeyed, skewed or silly could become engagingly quirky and refreshing once you know more about it. You may have miscalculated a few things, too. Maybe you thought your wife liked pasta dishes, only to find out that the only part she likes about pasta is making you happy. That would make a difference if pasta were on the menu every other day.

Try these questions:

How were your growing-up experiences different from mine? Tell me about one aspect. Now, you may know quite a lot about your spouse's childhood, adolescence, adulthood—his or her experiences before you were married. Yet you will never know it all. Even your mate will have sudden remembrances, flashbacks of experiences long forgotten.

Did your parents relate to you in ways that you think differed from the ways in which my parents related to me? Your parents influenced you in your early years—you learned values and cultural mores from them. They provided you with standards. When you were young, you saw much of the world around you through their eyes. How do you suppose the roles your parents played affect your role and the role you expect your mate to take?

What kinds of activities did you participate in after school when you were in high school? How were they different from mine? You realize now how much you have to learn about each other. For you to know how your mate's experiences differed from your own, you have to know what those experiences were.

Did your church have a good youth program, and were you a part of it? How was that different from my experience? You and your mate may have altogether different church backgrounds. You may have attended a two-thousand-member, inner-city church with youth programs galore, cramming activities in from morning until night every day of the week. Your mate may have attended a twenty-member rural church whose pastor was responsible for two or three area churches. In all likelihood, the only youth group available outside of public school would have been a 4-H Club. Considering this difference alone, you could assume that your partner did not have as much opportunity for Christian fellowship and training as you did.

How did your family's devotional time differ from my family's? Did you have regular family devotions? If you did, what were they like? Who led them? Were they always the same? Did you enjoy them? How did they affect your spiritual life? Since it is important for you to grow together spiritually, you both need to know what opportunities you have had as well as how you have used those opportunities.

Tell me about your best friends. Who were they, and what were they like? Where are they now? How are they different from my best friends? What was it about them that you liked that differed from my friends? Knowing what kinds of friends your mate chose will tell you something, perhaps, about what your mate likes about you. Friends are drawn together by mutual interests, goals and gifts (such as athletic skills, music, art and literature). You may learn that your mate has been suffering from the neglect of interests and activities that were once very important to her or to him. You may also learn that some of the things your mate would enjoy, you could learn to enjoy.

Share the grand successes, the embarrassments, the failures, the deplorable, the negative with the positive. After all, your responses to life events communicate who you are. The questions you can ask in the *Discovering Differences* game will be as infinite, varied and meaningful as you make them. They will become more interesting as you get better at asking questions and responding, as you grow to know each other over the months and years, as your interests develop and your love deepens. This is one game with real dividends, and both of you will be winners. The fragments, the impressions, what seemed to be contradictory messages, the little or not-so-little misconceptions, will be replaced with portraits. As your game skills sharpen, the portraits will sharpen from abstract to impressionistic to realistic. You will never see each other as intimately, with as much care, love and compassion as your Creator sees you, yet you will know each other better than you know anyone else. You cannot help but love someone who cares enough to want to know all about you and is willing to share all of himself or herself with you in return.

Several years ago my wife and I attended a three-day seminar for married couples, and there we were instructed to inventory the elements that composed our love. Midway through the weekend I realized again why I had first fallen in love with my wife. She was lovable, and she was—and is—my beloved. Oh, how refreshing that single weekend experience was! Think what your own investiture of time for sharing will do for you and your mate. Getting inside of each other, feeling the pain and the joy, will create a kindred spirit, a oneness almost too difficult to analyze and express. But be curious about your mate, not about yourself.

There is an issue that I want to stress once more before closing this chapter, and that is the importance of talking together. Unless you talk together, you cannot be emotionally intimate. If you woo and forget, you will woo, forget and *lose,* too. Before your neglect of each other precipitates a showdown, double your attention to each other.

Now, please allow me to ask you some direct questions. Ladies first.

Do you, as wife, know the pressures your husband feels when an attitude adjustment toward priorities is necessary? He has responsibilities, sometimes overwhelming responsibilities, at work, financially, spiritually, at home and socially. How is he going to weed through and prioritize them successfully? Do you understand the guilt feelings he has when he cannot be at home with you and the children as much as he would like? Do you understand the stress that his work environment places on him?

Husband, this is your turn. Are you in tune with your wife's pressures: the children's wants and needs, the endless cleaning, cooking, laundry, chauffeuring, the career she may be trying to balance with responsibilities at home, as well as attempting to meet your desires and needs? Do you understand her need to talk to you, to spend time with you? Do you understand her monthly menstrual cycle that may cause her to draw away from you? Do you understand her need for family and friends? Do you understand why she becomes "emotional"?

You both can understand, you know. Browse through this chapter one more time because when you learn to play the question-and-answer games quite well, you will experience the mutual challenge and delight of winning at the ultimate game of togetherness: *intimacy*.

As you work on the differences and similarities in your marriage relationship, be well aware that you are beginning to *understand* each other better. Whenever you allow yourself to be vulnerable to anyone, you must also be able to *trust* each other.

Out on a Limb for Your Mate

A Case for Vulnerability and Trust

*I*t was obvious: Will was not going to make it in the class, and I had to tell him. He had enrolled in a graduate course I was teaching at a state hospital in the northeast. It was not because he was not smart enough to do well. Due to the nature of the class, students had to be vulnerable to a process that went on for the duration of the summer term. They had to be honest, open and communicative about their feelings while relating to peers and supervisors. Will could not seem to do it. His fellow students worked him over to no avail, and finally he protested their interference.

When he and I sat down to appraise the situation, he broadsided me, "You are not going to get me to open up anything I don't want to!" Considering his flushed face and rapid breathing, I tended to agree with him. He seemed to feel that he had much to protect, and the pressure of supervisors and students made him feel too vulnerable. He could not cope.

Even his explanation was guarded. When he calmed down enough to talk, he said simply, "I don't like to say good-byes." Will's fear was based on a healthy assumption that sharing himself with someone would gradually move the relationship toward a bonding friendship. He knew that developing friendships was a very real possibility in that course, and because of his potential for clinging to others and fear of letting them go, he did not want to take any risk at all. I recollect the painful moment when he withdrew, knowing that he would receive an "incomplete" for the course. The closest he came to accepting vulnerability was the moment he left us, tears running down his reddened cheeks. He could have re-entered the course, but he chose to leave.

Vulnerability threatens everyone. We are all vulnerable to something or to someone sometime in our lives. Most of us remember feeling vulnerable to newly awakened sexual impulses when we were teens. Some of us may have felt vulnerable to supervisors' attacks, perhaps to teachers who berated our academic efforts. Inevitably when we place our skills or feelings before others, we accept the risk of being criticized.

Preachers, plumbers, news anchormen, county assessors, violinists, figure skaters and junior-high wrestlers risk exposing their skills to scrutinizing groups. Any general contractor who has had to be licensed and bonded realizes the potential for criticism. People want to receive positive responses. The kind of response received could very well determine whether or not an individual will perform at his or her best in the future. If the response is ridicule, an actor may stumble over his lines or leave the stage (hopefully not dodging eggs). Positive reinforcement encourages repetitive attempts at fulfilling the need for personal acceptance; it encourages risk-taking. A negative response does the opposite; it encourages risk-avoiding.

No one grows without vulnerability. No one becomes any better at anything that can be seen, heard or otherwise detected without the potential for comments. When learning a new skill, our first attempts are awkward; but with practice, we can repeat the procedure with less effort and concentration. Standards, whether realistic or unrealistic, are always around us. Look to the left, then to the right. You are bound to find someone who has an idea of good, better and best... or fair, worse and worst, as the case may be. If you are going to attempt to achieve a goal and draw attention in the process, you are going to be vulnerable.

If you find critical observations by others hard

to manage, is it not only logical to hide your skills? That depends. What are the rewards versus the risks? Now think of the opposite situation. If you can be criticized, you can also criticize. What effect does your criticism have on your mate? If you snicker at your mate's feeble attempts at communicating feelings and maintain that negative attitude, your mate will eventually withdraw from you. Anyone would become disheartened by constant insensitivity or complaining.

Who is more vulnerable than a mate? Who knows you any better than your mate knows you? Who is more qualified to take a crack at you than your mate? Whose opinion means more to you than your mate's? When someone is well-acquainted with the foibles and follies of your personality, is it not tempting to retreat into yourself for fear that what looks bad is probably even worse and the more you were to say, the more trouble you would get into?

Can you imagine how hard it would be for a turtle to withstand the pounding, bouncing, tossing and gnawing of a determined bear? To hold itself inside the shell would take all the turtle's strength. People get tired just thinking about a potential pounding, so they scrunch up inside their shells and shiver.

Whether you are being tossed by circumstances or people or only trying to ward off possible distress, you need to be aware of your weaknesses, and you need to make your mate aware of them, too. If fear of vulnerability inhibits you from close relationships, you will constantly feel threatened; but at the very moment that you make the decision to risk being vulnerable to your mate, you will be at a positive turning point. Believe me, taking the risk *for* and *with* your mate is worth a try...it is worth many tries. "Confess your sins to each other and pray for each other so that you may be healed" (James 5:16) not only makes spiritual sense, it makes therapeutic sense.

Digging up the roots of your fears and exposing them to sunlight and air will help dry them out. Fears can rot, you know, and become ever-greater problems. The spade that cuts through to the base of those roots is sharp, and it can hurt, but the hurt is part of the healing. The more trust that you invest in your mate and the more often you share your weaknesses, the sooner the hurt will lessen.

There is giving with the taking and taking with the giving, too. The way you handle your mate's weaknesses is just as important as the way your mate handles yours. You are dealing with a fragile part of the ego when you hear and take to heart the priceless expressions of vulnerability. Respect encourages trust, and solemn assurances of respect and confidentiality align with a positive relationship.

Respect and confidentiality are necessary elements of the marriage commitment. You gain and hold those elements by listening intently, creatively, with your undivided attention; by saying *thank you* when something, when anything is done for you; by showing appreciation for little as well as big things shared between you; by saying reassuring words like "I love you" even though that could be assumed; by giving compliments that you genuinely feel; by crying unashamedly or quietly sitting with your tearful mate in support; and by being willing to share a fault, weakness or error with confidence and to listen without judgment as your partner reciprocates.

Any step toward intimacy will be doubled in length and value when taken with your mate. The more prolonged the time you take to be with your mate, the more concern, respect and honor you show, the richer and more profound your rewards will be. Take the risk of being vulnerable. Let your partner be vulnerable, too. Without the courage to take that risk, you will neither know nor be known. If your courage is like a wave in the Pacific surf, ride its first crest, great or small.

You realize, of course, that you are going to have to go beyond Kirkegaardian leap-in-the-dark risk-taking when you share yourself with your partner. Eventually you will have to place your trust in him or her.

> "Oh the comfort, the inexpressible comfort, of feeling safe with a person, having neither to weigh thoughts nor measure words, but pouring them all right out, just as they are, chaff and grain together; certain that a faithful hand will take and sift them, keep that which is worth keeping, and then with the breath of kindness, blow the rest away."

So said Dinah Maria Mulock Craik (1826-1887), expressing the sentiment we all feel when we are with a kindred spirit. How blessed we are when that friend is our marriage partner!

All of us, at one time or another, have shared confidences with someone we did not know in the slightest, almost as though that person were judge or jury. When a stranger reserves his opinions and categorizations to himself, we are inclined to exploit the arrangement, hoping to present a favorable case for ourselves with little or no hindrance. Unfortunately, a stranger has no quarrel, much less a qualified judgment, because he has scant interest other than curiosity or basic human sympathy. Only someone who has a stake in the case will be interested enough to take a viable role.

New counselees often ask me (in their own way and typically indirectly) if they can trust me. They test and question. They pose hypothetical problems. Whatever and however they ask me, they understandably do not intend to share their problems with me, a perfect stranger to them, until they receive my assurance that I will keep what they say confidential. If I am to be of any help, and if we are ever to get to the business at hand, I have to help them trust me. Developing trust takes time. Counselees repeatedly test, prod and evaluate. If all goes well, the relationship will become spontaneous and positive. But if I blow it just once, the whole process will have to begin again, only with much more difficulty and far more effort.

Developing trust in a marriage relationship is similar to that of counselor and counselee, but the process begins with a mutual commitment and objective. I am not going to delude you into thinking that trust is easily come by, nor that it is easily maintained. Trust requires intense desire and the unrelenting investment of two people in each other. At some point, we all have to determine for ourselves whether or not a particular relationship is worth our commitment. But the marriage relationship deserves the best commitment, the best effort.

In the heat of an argument, a marriage partner is apt to exclaim, "Why don't you leave me if you think I am so hard to live with?" One partner I know responded, "Because I am committed to our marriage." She did not say she was committed to her husband, but she was committed to their marriage. She was not feeling cozy thoughts about him at all, yet she was willing to stand by the man she had committed her life to during a less infuriating moment. She was focusing on what their marriage could become in the future.

Responsible commitment is reflected in the words most of us included in our wedding ceremonies: "in sickness and health," "till death do us part" and "forsaking all others." If we meant what we vowed then, we should still mean what we vowed then.

How can we learn to trust? We learn to do it by doing it. We can get better at trusting. The recipe for trust is consistency pressed together by tenacity and seasoned with time. No matter how much stress is involved in the relationship—through illness, financial losses, misunderstanding, catastrophes of any kind—the wedding vows are the basis for a formidable trust that can be counted on forever.

Let me ask you this: Can you rectify a broken commitment? That is a very important question, and you need to address its implications. Do you recall the Old Testament story of Hosea and Gomer? Hosea was a prophet of the Northern Kingdom of Israel who God asked to marry a prostitute. Hoping for the best, Hosea fell in love with Gomer and made the marriage contract. It did not take long for him to realize that Gomer would not be exclusively his, and she left him for other men. Then God told Hosea to look for her and try to win her back. In spite of Gomer's adulterous liaisons, Hosea persisted and eventually they were remarried.

Hosea and Gomer's tragic experiences paralleled those of God and the nation of Israel. Israel turned away from God and worshiped the baals and other gods of Canaan instead. The result was Israel's temporary exile in Babylon, after which the repentant people returned to God and found His loving acceptance. If you found yourself in a similar tough situation, could you make the necessary effort to reclaim your mate? Could you, like Hosea, do it with God's help? In the closing chapter, God says of His people, "I will heal their waywardness and love them freely..." (Hosea 14:4).

Unfortunately, one tragedy can lead to another, even worse tragedy unless the cheated-on partner follows Hosea's example. Frank, a paraplegic with children of his own, married Joanne, a woman twenty-five years his junior, and they nobly vowed to love each other until the end of time. In spite of Frank's handicap, which prevented a satisfying sexual consummation of their love, they cared for and loved each other.

Under her husband's direction, Joanne capably managed his small variety store. When the workload became too heavy, Frank hired assistants for her. One of those assistants very sympathetically listened to her and encouraged her to cry on his shoulder. Eventually, with her permission, he crawled into bed with her. Through the employees' grapevine, Frank accidentally found out what happened and forced Joanne to confess what she had done.

For the next few days, Frank leafed through the Bible used in their wedding ceremony, searching for comforting and reassuring words to help him hold back his natural striking reflex. He felt inclined to destroy Joanne, and both knew that and were afraid. Anything either said became a threat to the other, until in a directionless argument, Joanne ran to the safety of a narrow doorway that Frank could not get through with his wheelchair. Her hands cupped her face, and sobs shook her body. Backing into the den, she reached for the gun that Frank kept loaded in case of a break-in. She checked the clip, pointed the gun at her temple, pulled the trigger and died while Frank stared helplessly through the doorway.

In a sense, Frank died with Joanne. No matter whose the blame was, or the greater or lesser blame, guilt was the issue they addressed, not forgiveness. Not rectification. Not reconcilement. Both Frank and Joanne were caught off-balance by the tragedy of a broken commitment. Neither realized that healing comes with brave hope, with persistent, maturing understanding, with time.

Sometimes a mate will frantically demand immediate, rectifying explanation or action, not realizing that restoration of balance and harmony in the marriage will require prodigious effort. There is no easy answer. There is no easy way out. What there *is* is injury and the need for healing. The broken commitment may be a visible symptom of a cancer that should have been tended to long ago, but somehow was ignorantly or callously left to spread. There was no sense of immediacy then. Why is it that the break of a commitment makes immediacy so important that it adds to the problem, making a solution almost impossible? John Lennon and Paul McCartney used to sing, "Yesterday, all my troubles seemed so far away," but the yesterdays cannot be reconstructed, at least not with the same naiveté.

Yet, new hope can be salvaged from broken promises, especially in Christian marriages. Hope, desire and determination—with God's help—will find a way. Once your relationship has suffered a crushed trust, more than anything else you need the Holy Spirit's assistance to soothe bruised egos. Can you change your attitude? Can your mate change his or her attitude alone? Few Christian mates believe that. Only a divine touch can thoroughly change attitudes, and you need to go to God for that touch.

Or maybe you think you could just forget what happened. Haven't you heard that before? "Forget it. Cheer up. Don't nag, don't be depressed, don't pout and whine. Just forget it." But, can a clandestine rendezvous be wiped clean from the record just by forgetting it? The price of that forgetting is *fear* that the commitment will be broken again when least expected. Better to be honest before hope dies.

If a commitment has been broken, before doing or saying anything, allow yourself to get over the initial shock. When the hurt has toned down to the extent that you can think, concentrate upon your partner. Never ever argue without listening. Give your undivided attention—as never before—to your partner. This emergency needs to be handled carefully, with as much clarity of mind as possible.

In order for trust to be reinstated, attention must be centered upon the offending mate. Watch for his or her body statements, words and phrasing, eye contact. Subtle clues give revealing evidences that will reinforce or correct your perception. Look for nervous tics, eyes that stare into the distance, shuffling feet, tapping fingers, disconnected words and phrases, diverted attention, yawning, anything that will help you understand your mate. If truth comes out, it will be by gentle, nurturing motioning into the light of scrutiny.

If you are the offending partner, do not run away. Do not hide in the shadows because the shadows will only make the truth more painful when it finally comes to light. It is possible that if you pull a cover-up, your mate will never discover your moment of unfaithfulness, but your unfaithfulness will continue simply in your living a lie. What you have done will have repercussions, you know. You may wonder if you'll be found out. You may even respect your partner less for being duped. You may show your irritations more, or you may become more "helpful" all of a sudden, more "loving." You may spend more money. Or, you may be tempted to stay with the third party who has put a wedge between you and your partner. Don't you see? You will be living an AWOL existence. You will never be free to be yourself until you honestly give yourself up to your partner.

Faithfulness sustains a marriage, making it possible for both of you to trust without worry, to give without exploiting, to feel without fear, to speak without lying. Why fret about the hidden dimensions of your life? When you have nothing to hide, you will be free to express yourself in all good faith, without dire consequences. By being the real you, integrity and faithfulness will naturally be yours. Your mate will have nothing to fear simply because you have made a responsible and honest commitment to restore your relationship.

Finally, learn to forgive as God will forgive you in Christ Jesus if you ask Him to. Forgiving is much better than forgetting. Learn to love as God loves you. Learn to give of yourself as Christ gave Himself for you at Calvary. Join your mate in prayer and Bible reading. Renew your interest in each other. There in God's presence, both of you will find healing and restoration.

There are times when the communication stream slows to a trickle and turns into an icy block—those miserable times when trust seems almost nonexistent. Do not give up! You can crack the ice. I want you to be aware of a problem-solving approach presented in the next chapter. Whether or not your relationship is in trouble, you can prepare for days of poor communication. You will find *The Seven Steps for Conflict Resolution* one of the most effective ways to break your way through the ice.

Sez Who?
The Seven Steps for Conflict Resolution

*H*ave you heard of a Sufi judge? You would not want to meet one in court. Here is the tale.[5]

Two men had an argument. To settle the matter, they went to a Sufi judge for arbitration. The plaintiff made his case. He was eloquent and persuasive in his reasoning, and when he finished, the judge nodded in approval and said, "That's right, that's right."

On hearing this, the defendant jumped up and said, "Wait a second, Judge, you haven't even heard my side of the case yet." So the judge told the defendant to state his case. And he, too, was very persuasive and eloquent. When he finished, the judge said, "That's right, that's right."

When the clerk of court heard this, he jumped up and said, "Judge, they both can't be right." The judge looked at the clerk of court and said, "That's right, that's right."

No one wins a fight if married to the loser. Both lose. Neither win. If both win, two lose.

Most marriage relationships need an occasional problem-solving technique to deal with conflict. Because of repetitive contact with the same partner day after day, a marriage is prone to countless minor skirmishes, impetuous insults, steamy sarcasm and character assassinations that can get out of hand. With harsh words ringing in his ears, a marriage partner is likely to withdraw in apparent indifference and turn cold shoulders to his mate—or worse, lose a grip on himself and slash back at the offender with irrational jabs.

Whether living, working or playing together, before too long one discovers that friendships, marriages, even business partnerships, can be threatened by misunderstandings. It is painful to watch a valued relationship deteriorate after a conflict because of defensiveness or lack of a workable procedure for restoring it.

I want to suggest to you a conflict resolution process that I call *The Seven Steps*.[6] The steps rest upon a theory that conflict resolution is possible when defensiveness is controlled and discussion about a conflict is organized. I have used *The Seven Steps* with many couples in marriage and family counseling at Renew, and with few exceptions, the procedure has begun a process of healing relationships and in some cases restored them completely. I do not expect *The Seven Steps* to cure most relationship problems. I do, however, expect it to begin a process of healing while exposing the factors and sources of the conflict to the persons involved. Keep in mind that this procedure is only the beginning of an on-going process of communication which could require the services of a trained counselor.

Before beginning *The Seven Steps,* you need to agree to abide by two rules included to help you successfully accomplish this exercise.

Rule One: *Face Each Other*

Some couples like to argue from one room to another, in front of a television or while riding in an automobile. As a result, they miss the opportunity to observe revealing clues. Facing each other helps us avoid tune-out, a plague on many relationships. Part of the communication process depends upon observing facial expressions and body movements.

Rule Two: *Do Not Interrupt*

This rule was added after several couples found that they could not state their cases without constant interruptions. When you feel defensive, you may tend to interrupt your mate, especially when you dislike what you hear about yourself. By interrupting, you imply that what you have to say is more important than what your mate has to say. To help control your interruptions while your mate is talking, pretend that tape is covering your mouth.

Note: Every step in *The Seven Steps* must be done in consecutive order, with each partner alternating at each step. For example, a married couple may choose to begin with the husband. He will begin by doing the first step and his wife following before he starts the second step, the third step, and so on.

Now, let us begin.

Step One: RESENTMENTS

"I resent...."

The first step provides you with an opportunity to share resentments you have about your mate. Most people find this the hardest step of all. It takes courage to be candid and truthful. Bring up every resentment you can think of. Like festering sores, resentments need to be lanced so that the poisonous build-up of anger can be released. When repressed, anger becomes resentment, and resentment settles into depression.

You will find it hard to listen to your mate share resentments about you. But remember this: The resentments you will hear will not be the resentments you feel toward yourself; they will be the resentments that your mate feels. You do not have to agree. Chances are you will not. Proving or even disproving the basis of a resentment is irrelevant and futile. Resentments do not always rest on facts. What is important is not what happened to cause the resentment, but that an impression was made causing anger to turn into resentment. It is not enough to tell the other person, "You should not feel that way." The fact is, he or she does feel that way. Because your mate's interpretation of an event is different from yours does not make either of you more right or wrong.

You may have two resentments about your mate, or you may have two hundred. The number of resentments does not really matter, but you need to acknowledge all of the resentments you have. You will be defusing the repression that turns resentments into depression.

Step Two: REGRETS

"I regret...."

The second step is usually more emotional; it is about feelings that make up your relationship. Tell your partner the issues, events, words or actions you regret having caused to happen. Tears may come, prompting you to stop. I encourage you to complete this step. It will reveal much about your relationship.

Remember, do not respond to your partner, but state your regrets and then listen.

Step Three: CONCERNS
(Based upon the past, as they affect the present.)
"I am concerned about...."

Our memories sometimes make it hard for us to forgive. We are prone to be wary of the person who has hurt or let us down. As a result, the restoration of trust comes slowly. For example, a husband was forced out of his home by court order because he physically abused his family. After treatment, he feels ready to go home, but his wife's concerns about him will include the possibility that the abuse will happen again. Her concern is based upon his history and affects how she sees the present relationship.

For negotiations to proceed toward resolution, you need to know why your mate sees hindrances to eventual restoration of the relationship. This step will give you the data to begin to change.

The first steps, now, have focused on the negative based upon the past. The next three are positive and future-oriented.

Step Four: FANTASY
"I want...."

You and your partner will probably enjoy this step more than the other six steps. Take this opportunity to let your spouse know what dreams or plans you have for your relationship. You might share a fantasy including a second honeymoon or a trip around the world with unlimited funds to lavish gifts on your mate, or perhaps a dream house for the two of you, or helping others through a special ministry. It does not matter how outlandish or trite your dreams or fantasies may seem or that you have not shared them before. By doing this, you will help your partner to see an imaginative side of you that may have been overlooked. Have fun with this step.

Step Five: MUST HAVE

"I need...."

Now you have the opportunity to tell your mate what—for you—constitutes the essentials of your relationship. These are the essentials you believe are necessary in order for your relationship to work and without which your relationship cannot work. Be precise and to the point. Then listen intently to what your partner says because the quality of your relationship and its possible improvement are contingent upon these essentials.

Step Six: CONTRACT

"I promise...."

In this step you have the opportunity to let your partner know what you have heard by responding with what you are willing to change. Do not promise more than you are willing to produce. Only that.

Caution: Do not write your promises down. Inevitably you, your partner or someone else will dig up the lists after a period of time in order to expose a breach of contract. Your contracting will be done in good faith. Do your best to deliver what you promise. It works both ways. Both of you are promising. You are not responsible to see that your partner lives up to his or her promises; that is your partner's business.

Step Seven: PRAYER

"Lord, help...."

In this final step, ask for God's help. Pray positively for your mate's work, health and well being—all of the needs you can think of. Do not request God to make changes in your partner; that would be judgmental. Instead, pray that God will help *you* to make necessary changes while working toward an improved relationship. Ask God to help you with everything that you and your mate do together.

If at any time during *The Seven Steps* you feel extremely uncomfortable, or if one of you cannot go on because of emotional stress, do not hesitate to contact a trained counselor. Request help for yourself if your relationship has not improved or has worsened after going through *The Seven Steps*. There is no shame in seeking help for your relationship, but there is shame indeed to need help and refuse to ask for it.

Solving relationship problems alone is nearly impossible. We often need the insight and objectivity of others. But as you will see in the next chapter, none of us began life with objective problem solving and the interaction that it requires.

The Love You Need
and the Conflict You Cannot Resolve Alone

*Y*ou and I were born without anyone *asking* us if we wanted to be born. No one *asked* us if we wanted to begin life as infants. We had no say as to who our parents would be, whether we would have brothers and sisters, when or where we would be born and what the outlook of our future would be. No one *asked us* anything at all. We were helpless babes when we were born, and we cried like everything in the birthing process.

Before long, we learned that our feelings could be hurt and that we wanted sensitive solace and care from others. We naturally looked for love because we were inadequate in ourselves. We were dependent upon others not only for food, clothing and shelter, but for emotional support. We were anxiously looking for love and did not know it.

A man incarcerated in a federal penitentiary is separate from free men and women. He feels, if his psyche has not been too distorted, his estrangement from people on the outside. But do you know that each one of us is separate from *all* the rest of God's creation? Our uniqueness makes us separate. Your genes and your particular circumstances make you separate from everyone else.

If you excel at something, you rise above some norm; if you fail, you fall below some expectation. If you have red hair and your peers have black hair, you are separate from your peers. The universe is wide and high and deep, with many beings in it. You are a small and insignificant creature next to the majestic humpback whale gliding through an Arctic estuary, breaching through the rigid ice in a single, effortless movement. You have neither Leviathan's size nor might. In all probability you are quite unable to communicate with the marine mammal, even to mimic its patterned song. You see, you are separate.

You have good reason to enjoy being separate, to know that no one is exactly like you; but your separateness can make you feel very, very alone. When Adam was in the Garden of Eden, all of his responsibilities and all of his diversions could not satisfy his need of someone else. The chroniclers of the Pentateuch reveal this fact in Genesis 2:20-22:

> *"For Adam no suitable helper was found.* So the Lord God caused the man to fall into a deep sleep; and while he was sleeping, he [God] took one of the man's ribs and closed up the place with flesh. Then the Lord God made a woman from the rib he had taken out of the man, and he brought her to the man."

Adam was separate from God, and he was separate from all of God's creation. That condition was serious enough for God to say, "It is not good for the man to be alone. I will make a helper suitable for him" (Genesis 2:18). Who was this helper to alleviate Adam's aloneness? Eve, our first mother. Adam needed Eve.

In this we are all alike: We all need someone to love, and we need to be loved in return. If we are an Adam, we need an Eve; if we are an Eve, we need an Adam. And like Adam and Eve, we need God.

What happens if we believe we have no one to love and no one to love us in return? Many things can happen, all of them negative but for the grace of God, who changes things. Some people who feel estranged, alone and unwanted in a hostile environment, feel trapped; but instead of breaking away, they seal the trapdoor from the inside and adjust to its confines. As they hide in their dark burrows, clutching what remnants of life outside they still value, their impression of reality loses its distinctness. In a sense, they lose their eyesight and their hearing. If forced out of seclusion to associate with free people, they panic and "escape" to the safety of their burrow behind the trapdoor. Their prison, to them, has become their sanctuary. Fortunately, they can be liberated if someone makes the arduous effort to free them.

Feelings of separateness and aloneness arouse a cold anxiety that withers an individual's self-confidence and sense of security. That same anxiety, like dry ice, will burn the fingers of anyone who tries the warm touch. As time passes and the freeze creeps deeper and deeper into a psyche, with no warmth of human love to thaw it, reaction time slows and the person falls into a form of death-in-life, a torpor truly separate from humanity and the Creator.

Adam and Eve knew the warmth of genuine love and mutual support that God had intended for them. When they experienced separation for the first time, it was through an act of defiance. God told them they could eat the fruit of every tree in the Garden with the exception of one, the "tree of the knowledge of good and evil" (Genesis 2:17). Ah, and the fruit of that tree was "pleasing to the eye" (Genesis 3:6). But there was something more to that fruit than beauty. God had said, "*when* you eat of it you will surely die," but the tempter hissed, "God knows that *when* you eat of it your eyes will be opened, and you will be like God, knowing good and evil" (Genesis 3:4). God knew that Adam and Eve would defy Him, that they would break the bond between Him and themselves that they could never mend alone. The harmony would be gone. For the first time, there was anxiety in Eden.

Did Adam and Eve become as wise as God? Well, then, did they become gods themselves? No, they simply recognized their separateness, aloneness and inadequacy in the eyes of their perfect and holy Creator. They saw that they were naked, and with a jolt, that they were different from each other. Eve felt manipulated by the tempter who had taken on the form of the serpent, the most crafty of the wild animals in the Garden. Adam felt manipulated by Eve who had given him the fruit to eat. And do you know, Adam confirmed his split from Eve when he denied his responsibility for her. Adam said, "The woman you [God] put here with me—she gave me some fruit from the tree, and I ate it" (Genesis 3:12). Determined not to bear all of the blame, Eve accused the serpent: "The serpent deceived me, and I ate" (Genesis 3:13). That was not a happy moment for anyone, except perhaps the tempter, who was no doubt making a quick exit, leaving the serpent he had used behind him. Satan had succeeded in separating the first human couple.

The first act of separation from the Holy One initiated the second act of separation from Him. Adam and Eve's firstborn son, Cain, attacked his brother, Abel, and with his savage blow, death entered human experience. Abel was separated from his grieving parents. Cain became "a restless wanderer on the earth" (Genesis 4:12). A calamity with almost endless repercussions occurred when Eve ate the fruit and did her husband a disservice by giving him the fruit to eat, too; when Adam ate that fruit in full knowledge of his disobedience to God; when Adam refused to defend Eve in order to cover for himself. The dominoes fell one by one as Adam and Eve learned the opposites of loyalty, unity, responsibility and love for each other. Hate became a reality, and death followed soon after.

Cacophony, discord, alienation, anxiety, hate and hurt altered Adam and Eve's life-style, and all of the Adams and all of the Eves who have followed in the millennia since have struggled to find the love they lost. They were and we are broken people. Only with God's help can we grow into the image of Christ, who was Love manifest in the flesh, and develop harmonious, loving relationships with the people around us.

The Way to Win

You see, the conflict and subsequent anxiety that began in the Garden of Eden is one war that we—neither you nor I—can win on our own. We are instructed to "be strong in the Lord and in his mighty power.... For our struggle is not against flesh and blood, but against the...powers of this dark world and against the spiritual forces of evil in the heavenly realms" (Ephesians 6:10,12). Could we hold the line against the powers of darkness without God's royal banner over us?

Nothing has changed since the tempter smuggled discord into Eden—nothing except God's plan of salvation that the tempter could not subvert in the Wilderness of Temptation or at the pinnacle of the Temple in Jerusalem; that the tempter could not prevent at Christ's resurrection from the grave, ascension into heaven and glorification at His Father's right hand; that the tempter could not destroy at Pentecost; that the tempter could not stem from spreading throughout the Roman Empire and finally to the farthest reaches of Earth.

Well, then, something wonderful has happened. What neither you nor I could do, God has done for us through His only begotten Son, Jesus Christ. He is knocking on the trapdoor of our burrow. If we let Him, He will break the trapdoor down and set us free to love and be loved. You remember John 3:16, don't you? Read it once again, but this time read the following verse as well.

> "For God so *loved* the world that he gave his one and only Son, that whoever believes in him shall not perish but have eternal life. *For God did not send his Son into the world to condemn the world, but to save the world through him.*"

Jesus Christ, who was conceived by the Holy Spirit and born of the virgin Mary, left His position of authority in heaven and became the second Adam. Son of God and Son of man, Jesus was as vulnerable—and as tempted—as you and I are, yet He did not fall victim to sin. He succeeded where the first Adam failed.

The Christ, the Savior of His own creation (Colossians 1:15,16), enjoyed the acceptance of a few people and suffered the rejection of most. He had devoted friends and determined enemies. Only one who is willing to offer himself honestly to others can know the joy of intimacy or the sorrow of a broken heart. Jesus knew both, but He considered the suffering worth the glory that was to come.

As the sacrificial Lamb, the unspotted, perfect Lamb of God, Jesus paid the highest ransom that anyone ever paid. He substituted His sinless life for the first Adam and for all of humanity then, now and to come. Only He could do it. He paid the price that neither you nor I could pay, and He did it on our behalf because He loved us. The price of sin is death and separation from God. On the Roman cross, high on the hill of Golgotha outside Jerusalem, Christ bore all of humanity's sins. His sacrifice made full atonement once and for all. He resolved the conflict triggered by Adam and Eve's disobedience.

In the last three hours of His lonely suffering, the sun eclipsed; and in the darkness, God the Father turned away from His Son. Christ was on the cross six hours, but when a soldier's spear pierced His side, He was already dead, probably of a ruptured, broken heart. *Our* sins separated Him from His Father.

Then came Easter morning.

When you give your heart to Christ and accept His atonement for your sins, the impenetrable wall between you and God will dissolve, and you will begin to learn the richness and fullness of life that He originally intended for Adam and Eve in Eden. With Christ, you can win the conflict that you could not resolve alone.

"Once you were alienated from God and were enemies in your minds because of your evil behavior. But now he has reconciled you by Christ's physical body through death to present you holy in his sight, without blemish and free from accusation—if you continue in your faith, established and firm, not moved from the hope held out in the gospel" (Colossians 1:21-23).

"Christ in you" is your "hope of glory" (Colossians 1:27). If God is on your side, you have a great future ahead—not just in this life, but for eternity. Your own Easter is coming. You can afford the courage to open yourself to people around you, and above all, open your heart to your mate. Once you have trusted God to break down the barriers that have kept you from His love, you will find that being vulnerable to others—in order to love them and be loved in return—will become easier for you and your anxiety and loneliness will progressively diminish.

Just before the Passover Feast, shortly before His crucifixion, "Jesus knew that the time had come for him to leave this world and go to the Father. Having *loved* his own who were in the world, he now showed them the full extent of his love" (John 13:1). Jesus washed His disciples' feet.

"'Do you understand what I have done for you?' he asked them. 'You call me "Teacher" and "Lord," and rightly so, for that is what I am. Now that I, your Lord and Teacher, have washed your feet, you also should wash one another's feet. I have set you an example that you should do as I have done for you'" (John 13:12-15).

A little later that evening, Jesus told His disciples, "My children, I will be with you only a little longer.... A new commandment I give you: *Love* one another. As I have loved you, so you must *love* one another. All men will know that you are my disciples if you love one another" (John 13:33-35). "My command is this: *Love* each other as I have loved you. Greater love has no one than this, that one lay down his life for his friends" (John 15:12,13).

Are you and I prepared to *love* others even to the point of death? Would you die for your mate if your sacrifice were necessary to save him or her? That is the ultimate love, you know: the love that will be a willing sacrifice for the beloved.

Let me tell you a story before I close this chapter about the love you need and conflict you cannot resolve alone. This happens to be a compilation of true stories centered on a children's mission in the Big Apple, representative of thousands of children. I have changed the names.

Sammy was 14 when his mother left him on a New York City street corner. He said, "Mama, no..." but she shook her head and said, "I can't take it anymore, Sammy." That was the last time he ever saw her. He had been abused by his father for as long as he could remember, and his mother had been unable to protect him. The only people who had ever shown him attention were the drug pushers and pimps who wanted something from him. Sammy was cold and hungry. He had not eaten for two days when a young couple stopped their car and went over to him. They took him to a Christian mission, fed him, washed and clothed him, and showed him the first real love he had ever known.

Do you think it was easy to convince Sammy that he was lovable or that he could trust anyone to love him? Do you suppose that Sammy could immediately accept the Gospel story of God's love that paid such a price to save him and give him a glorious future? No, of course not. Sammy could not understand. He hurt, and he was afraid, and he thought the whole world was against him.

Now let me tell you something about that young couple who helped him to overcome his hurt and construct a meaningful future. They were part of a small cadre of Christians who had answered God's call to help children in inner New York City. They had paid a price to help. Two of them had been murdered. Two had been raped. Others had been stabbed. Another's jaw had been broken. Yet, they intended to fulfill their calling *for the duration.*

You see, some of them had been in Sammy's place. Loving Christians had helped them, and the deep hurt that those Christians helped to heal had turned into a love that would not quit in the face of opposition. New York City is resistant to God's love, but God's love is there still in the hearts of His children—the Sammys who count their suffering worth the glory to come. Your experiences are different, but you are a Sammy, too. You need Jesus. And you need to reach out to other people, especially your mate, for the healing that only love can bring. Then you need to help the Sammys you see all around you... and especially the Sammy who is your mate.

Hot, Cold or Ho-hum

What Does Sex Have to Do With Intimacy?

*H*ealthy marital partners enjoy the kind of love that everyone needs and should not have to do without: love for each other as *persons*. But for them, within the realm of marriage, this love is symbolized by a union that is sexual in nature but deeply emotional and spiritual in meaning.

King Solomon's book, after his name, is a love poem. It is the story of a powerful Mideastern king who chose a lovely young country maiden to be his bride. Read the following excerpts from Genesis to see for yourself if the Song of Solomon affirms God's blessing upon the sexual relationship between a husband and his wife.

Genesis

"God created man in his own image, in the image of God he created him; male and female he created them. God blessed them and said to them, 'Be fruitful and increase in number...'" (1:27,28), and "God saw all that he had made, and it was very good" (1:31).

Song of Solomon

Bride: "Let him kiss me with the kisses of his mouth—for your love is more delightful than wine" (1:2). "Take me away with you—let us hurry! The king has brought me into his chambers [bedroom]" (1:4).

Groom: "My dove in the clefts of the rock, in the hiding places on the mountainside, show me your face, let me hear your voice; for your voice is sweet, and your face is lovely" (2:14).

Bride (to herself): "All night long on my bed I looked for the one my heart loves" (3:1). "I found the one my heart loves. I held him and would not let him go..." (3:4).

Groom: "How beautiful you are, my darling! Oh, how beautiful! Your eyes behind your veil are doves..." (4:1). "Your lips are like a scarlet ribbon; your mouth is lovely" (4:3). "All beautiful you are, my darling; there is no flaw in you" (4:7). "How delightful is your love, my sister, my bride! How much more pleasing is your love than wine, and the fragrance of your perfume than any spice!" (4:10).

Bride: "My heart began to pound for him. I arose to open for my lover..." (5:4,5). "His mouth is sweetness itself; he is altogether lovely. This is my lover, my friend..." (5:16).

Groom: "You are beautiful, my darling.... Turn your eyes away from me; they overwhelm me" (6:4,5). "Your graceful legs are like jewels..." (7:7).

Bride: "I belong to my lover, and his desire is for me" (7:10). "Let us go early to the vineyards to see if the vines have budded, if their blossoms have opened, and if the pomegranates are in bloom—there I will give you my love" (7:12).

Whatever the point of this story is—the relationship of God and His Chosen, the Jews; the relationship of Christ and His Bride, the Church; or simply the beautiful, sensuous song of a man's love for his beloved—Solomon's Song goes beyond biology, beyond physical attractiveness, to character and to honest and intimate love.

To the king and his Shulamite maiden, the sexual expression of love is a blessing. In his letter to the Jewish Christians in Rome, a New Testament church leader wrote, "Marriage is honorable in all, and the bed undefiled" (Hebrews 13:4, *KJV*). God is not embarrassed about sex; it was His idea.

In full accord with Paul's instructions in Philippians 4:8, marital sex becomes the consummation, the fulfillment of two lovers' joyful, tender desire to give to each other and to receive from each other. Paul wrote, "Whatsoever things are true, whatsoever things are honest, whatsoever things are just, whatsoever things are pure, whatsoever things are lovely, whatsoever things are of good report; if there be any virtue, and if there be any praise, think on these things" (*KJV*). To the lover, his beloved is true, honest, just, pure, lovely, of good report, virtuous and worthy of praise. How can he help but think about her! And God understands that and approves.

At the same time, marital sex without justice, purity, loveliness and thoughts of good report, sex without consideration for personal virtue and praiseworthy intentions, the inappropriate and abusive use of it merits God's wrath. When sexual feelings are expressed under those conditions, they create guilt feelings, anger, hurt and condemnation that damage and destroy the marriage relationship.

Sex Is Not a Dirty Joke

When his wife criticized him for being too sexually oriented, the husband retorted in mock dismay, "And I haven't even been to Japan!" Humor is, perhaps, the most commonly used ploy to get around a serious discussion of sex. Sex triggers inhibitions like few other topics of life. Presumably there is enough embarrassment to avoid forthright, honest, mature interaction. Is fear the cause of this embarrassment or sense of propriety?

Humor, anger, anxiety, fear and stress revolve around this most personal of concerns in marriage.

To some, sex is ultra-important; nothing is more satisfying than their sexual experience. Some couples are hung up on sex, hungering for adequate physical relief they feel has been missing. Yet they cannot talk about it, at least not in a problem-solving way. Even if a man is bitter enough to make sex the subject of a coarse jest, he will often freeze into silence when approached with the opportunity to discuss the matter seriously. Ironically, the ones who guffaw loudest in the locker room, declaring or implying their sexual exploits, are often timid when it comes to discussion. For them, humor relieves the tension.

"I would rather have all the risks which come from free discussion of sex than the great risks we run by conspiracy of silence," wrote C. G. Lang, the archbishop of Canterbury. As a matter of fact, healthy sex has earned the silent treatment from much of the Church and large factions of society, I suppose to shield its abuses from juvenile and adult innocents.

Now in the twentieth century, secular society practically deifies sex, or more accurately, deifies *lust*. Marketing executives advertise consumer goods in suggestive packaging, such as phallic cologne bottles, promoted by more-or-less sexually explicit TV commercials. "Who is sexy?" they ask. Of course—whoever uses their products is sexy. But *lust* and *sex* as God meant it to be are two different subjects: One is negative, the other is positive. By tantalizing selfish desire and neglecting the attitude of agapé love (spontaneous, honest, self-giving, altruistic love), advertisers distort the impression of what love can be. They limit love to a narrow philosophy of selfish gratification that is opposed to this scriptural injunction:

> "Do nothing out of selfish ambition or vain conceit, but in humility consider others better than yourselves" (Philippians 2:3), and "Your attitude should be the same as that of Christ Jesus: who, being in very nature God, did not consider equality with God something to be grasped, but made himself nothing, taking the very nature of a servant, being made in human likeness. And being found in appearance as a man, he humbled himself and became obedient to death—even death on a cross!" (Philippians 2:5-8).

The humanistic, *me* philosophy and suppression of agapé love through silence have done more harm than we could imagine. Advertisers, of course, reflect buying habits and target audiences. Sales perpetuate and determine advertising methods.

If I am going to help you with your marriage relationship, I cannot justify neglecting the subject of sex, that tangible expression of affection between marriage partners. We refer to sexual encounters as "making love." Indeed, they should be in love, expressing love. Often, however, making love is nothing more than two writhing bodies with heartbeats and breathing rhythms elevated for the single purpose of achieving the epitomized orgasmic release.

Healthy sexual attitudes are necessary for a happy, satisfying marital relationship. Do you remember where you first picked up your attitudes about sex? Your parents may have avoided the issue, perhaps altogether, in your developmental years. Possibly you did not learn about sex until you looked into the subject yourself. Some experience a sexual encounter before they learn about it and far sooner than they are emotionally prepared for it. The result could be confusion as to sexual role and even identity, and consequently, sex could become associated with shame and fear.

I remember vividly when, as an adolescent boy, I meandered through the halls and rooms of the Toledo Art Museum unattended by an adult. Detached from the school group I had come with, I was enjoying my stay. In one of the rooms, I spied the representation of a nude hanging shamelessly above my head in a gilded frame. Her body, abandoned to the elements with only a shawl draped over her shoulders, was plumpish, pink and round. I was enchanted. Slowly I steadied myself on the couch positioned in the middle of the room. Lost in reverie, I relaxed my guard. Suddenly the whole room echoed with snickers and laughter. My classmates had caught me off guard. They had tried to watch me unnoticed until one of them broke out with a nose laugh and all was a-howl. My face reddened to crimson. I had been caught looking at a painting of a *nude*. That I would never live down. Shame, shame, *shame!*

Sexual feelings can also conjure fear of the unknown, of the forbidden fruit, even fear of sexual performance. Fear can disable a person so that he or she either does not dare to make friends or quickly drops casual friendships if startled by an attempt to deepen the relationship. Often, when a person's anxiety peaks, his sexual performance begins to wane; in reverse, when a person's confidence peaks, his sexual performance reflects that positive attitude, becoming more and more satisfying. Anxiety can inhibit sexual responses, and sexual responses can foster anxiety.

Ah, and then there is the guilt, the cutting edge of negative compliance often used to manipulate and control a partner while appearing to be personally exemplary. Many people have been told that they ought to feel guilty simply because of their natural sexual inclinations. If they believe that, they sometimes swing to the opposite pole of the pendulum arc and become sexually frigid.

Christians are occasionally Victorian in attitude even now in the twentieth century, prudish about sex, elevating mind over matter, soul over body, spiritual over material, as though God's temple were not our own flesh and blood but something ethereal and other-worldly. From that point of view, the idea of Christians as sexual beings cannot be entirely tolerated, although obviously the Victorian period in history produced its share of descendants. Instead of openly discussing healthy sex, the Victorian Christian zealously attacks lascivious sex. In so doing, he or she infers by default an uncomfortable dislike for one of God's ideas—healthy sex—initiated at the dawn of time.

A series of sermons on the positive side of sex would help to relieve undeserved guilt feelings among parishioners of all persuasions. What better place for healthy sex to be endorsed than in God's house and by one of God's own ambassadors? The tasteful, supportive proclamation of its attributes would testify to the glory of God's total creation.

Oneness

At the beginning of human history, an incredible thing happened. God designed two people, one of each sex, to become *one*. In the Garden of Eden, in the little paradise on earth, under the best conditions man will experience until the Second Coming of Christ, Adam said of Eve, "'This is now bone of my bones, and flesh of my flesh; she shall be called "woman," because she was taken out of man.' For this reason a man will leave his father and mother and be united to his wife, and they will become one flesh" (Genesis 2:23,24).

Thousands of years later, teachers of Judaic law brought the issue of divorce to Jesus. He would not satisfy them by condoning divorce even though they referred to Moses. Instead, He said, "They are no longer two, but one. Therefore what God has joined together, let not man separate.... Moses permitted you to divorce your wives because your hearts were hard. But it was not this way from the beginning" (Matthew 19:6,8).

In Paul's letter to the Christians at Corinth (a city with a bad reputation), he sharply warned against adultery and reaffirmed Genesis 2:23,24: "Do you not know that he who unites himself with a prostitute is one with her in body? For it is said, 'The two will become one flesh'" (I Corinthians 6:16).

The words of the Lord are reiterated once again in the Gospel of Mark: "At the beginning of creation God 'made them male and female.' 'For this reason a man will leave his father and mother and be united to his wife, and the two will become one flesh.' So they are no longer two, but one. Therefore what God has joined together, let man not separate" (Mark 10:6-9).

Back in my twenties, how two people could become one person baffled me. Then in a university course called "Human Sexual Behavior," obviously not philosophically designed to integrate the spiritual man with the physical, I began to understand. While the professor rattled on from his secular perspective, I thought of the miraculous process of birth and growth that God had designed.

An egg fertilized in the mother's womb contains all the genetic guidance a person will ever have. The sexual destiny of that person is already established although you cannot see it. If you measured two male and female fetuses side-by-side in their mother's womb six weeks after conception, you still could not observe any differences. In fact, the male fetus resembles the female at this early stage. They are one in appearance.

Then at six weeks old, their genes trigger differentiation and each fetus will develop either male or female characteristics. Slowly the penis becomes more external on the male fetus, and the corresponding part of the female anatomy becomes more internal, transforming into the clitoris. For each part of the male, a complementary part develops in the female.

The ovaries of the female have their counterpart in the testicles of the male; the labia, or outer lips of the vaginal canal, correspond to the scrotum of the male. The uterus within the female has its opposite in the prostate of the male.

These marvelous intrauterine physical developments called male or female babies begin from *one* similar but hard-to-detect life source in the bosom of their mothers. Slowly emerging to become distinct but nearly alike physical identities, they later meet as *one* in the marriage bed, with God's creative hand upon their union. This ultimate communion is not unlike the Lord's Supper which joins Christ, the Bridegroom, with His Church, His Bride, in the mystical union of spiritual *oneness*.

Oneness and Separation From Mom and Dad

Becoming one also involves separation. It means cutting apron strings. It means changing priorities. Priorities of other people and other responsibilities become secondary to the marriage relationship, to the union of marriage partners, to the oneness of the two individuals who are now man and wife.

All of us, male and female, need a special kind of nurturance to thrive in a relatively hostile world. We need love from our parents to build confidence and self-esteem, the kind of love that strengthens our trust in others. This love, this closeness, this nurturing relationship, this is *symbiosis*. You can see symbiosis in the way a mother cares for her newborn.

She can distinguish her baby's cry from another's almost immediately, and she soon learns to interpret the faintest differences in tone, gestures and facial expression.

Nine months of pregnancy begin the process. Some pregnant mothers sing lullabies to their unborn children. They watch their diets carefully to ensure their babies' good health. They break bad habits, smoking or drinking, whatever, habits that they would never have thought they could overcome before they learned that they were to be mothers. They pore over dictionaries of names; oh, how important the name is for a child. They strain to imagine what the future will be like when their children have grown into adults. You realize, that is just the beginning of their symbiotic relationship.

The day comes when a child is born. The umbilical cord fastened to his waist indicates that his union with his mother is a sturdy one. When the cord is severed, there remains an emotional attachment that, unfortunately, many mothers are unable to relinquish. Have you noticed how similar the word *mother* is to the word *smother*? Some mothers cannot seem to allow their children to grow up. For that matter, some fathers find it very difficult to let go of a son or daughter. The delicate balance between meeting the symbiotic needs of a child while encouraging his maturity can be a formidable task.

There have been times when I have teased one of my children, "You are growing too fast. Slow down. I cannot keep up with you." When they are little, children are so cute, adorable, lovable, dependent. But I know, as you do, that even if I could restrain their growing, to do so would be selfish. Like Peter Pan, they would be imprisoned in a Never Never Land, my own fantasy world. Their dependency would grow. Their problem solving and natural creativity would be severely impaired. If they allowed me to continue to determine their potential and limitations, they would forfeit their future for my sake. In the final analysis, neither I nor they would benefit.

They must be emancipated from my sovereignty. They need to draw up and sign their own declaration of independence. They have to set up their own congress and system of jurisprudence. Now, I would hope that what they have learned from my example would be reflected in all of that and that it would have given them a solid foundation upon which to build. I look forward to their being strong and healthy on their own. I will take pride in their self-sufficiency. When they are as free to grow and develop and succeed in God's eyes, under His watchful care and guidance, as they can be, then I will have satisfied my God-given appointment as their father.

Whether boy or girl, at some point a child must be freed from parents and home; yet, the process differs between boys and girls. A son must break with the influence of his mother earlier than a daughter does.

The daughter's trauma of separation comes when she leaves home to make another home, perhaps with a husband. Of course, a woman may feel unable to break free from her parents. Few women who have been over-protected—or at the other extreme, abused and neglected—function with healthy independence when they leave the nurturing nest. Their inexperience in managing stress, vocations, children, budgets and other responsibilities results in repeated failures and growing resentment. Extremes in parenting always leave their mark.

In his earliest years, a son is dependent upon his mother and spends most of his time with her; so, like a female child, he is usually closer to his mother than to his father. Eventually he will begin to follow his father's role model, often as a rival for the affections of his mother. How his parents deal with this sometimes-traumatic role jump can strengthen or destroy him.

If his mother turns to her male child for affection rather than to her husband, she may meet her needs at her child's expense. If his father turns to him for affection rather than to his wife, he may deprive his child of a normal relationship with a feminine figure and a healthy marital example. The boy needs both. Most of all, the child needs to recognize that his mother and father are committed to each other. Out of necessity, he should conclude, "If you can't beat 'em, join 'em," and break the bond with his mother, freeing himself to take on more masculine characteristics, which he sees in his father.

Some make the jump from their mothers to their fathers successfully. Others miss the mark and struggle with sexual identity. A male child has to reach the point where he says, in essence, "No, Mother, I do not want to be like you when I grow up. I want to be like Dad." If he does not, he will look for a woman to coddle and defend him like his mother did, cower from relationships and responsibilities, or make a show of bravado to scare potential threats away. He may accept the attentions of another male. Or, out of desperation, he may imitate the macho or violent male characters he sees on the video screen or the roughest men in his environment, stifling the fear inside that he will not make it as a legitimate adult male. He might even think that weightlifting, achieving a black belt in karate or skydiving would prove to others that he is a self-sufficient, adult male. At any rate, he will be at a disadvantage when squared off by the challenges of life.

"My husband will not tell me his feelings."

When a woman marries a man with dependency needs, both will be frustrated. Elevated for years by his mother, the husband will be determined to retain all of the rights and privileges of a feudal lord now that he is married. To do that, he must subjugate his wife to the status of feudal servitude; literally, he must make her his serf by taking away her freedom. He will carry a "big stick" and if she objects, pick up a bigger stick. His fear is that if she realizes that he is the slightest bit unsure of himself, he will lose it all; all the power and glory will be gone and the positions will be reversed. Because of the unfairness of that arrangement, he could be right.

When a heterosexual male's sexual identity is unclear to him, when the issue of dependency has not been resolved, he will have an inordinate drive to express his masculinity. But this expression amounts to *no* expression if he considers the expression of feelings to be a feminine characteristic. What was already an unstable marital relationship worsens without communication.

Some men in that situation claim they do not have feelings. Their blood pressure can soar, they can sweat, but they cannot feel anything. Oh, they actually do have feelings. They can hurt emotionally as well as physically, but they are determined not to show any weakness, any trait that could be interpreted as feminine. What catastrophe might happen if they were to admit that they have not dealt with a smothering parental relationship? They do not know and do not want to find out. No adult male wants to be thought of as a mama's boy.

Rosie Greer, 300 lb. former New York Giants and Los Angeles Rams pro football player, has been known to sit unabashedly on TV talk shows with needlepoint in hand—yes, needlepoint, a diversion usually thought of as reserved for the ladies. Rosie is not intimidated by any question of femininity. Not having to prove anything to anyone, be the discriminator male or female, he pursues his own interests.

Men and Women Have Needs in Common, But There Are Differences, Too

Valid or not depending upon point of view, changing or apparently stable, certain characteristics are considered masculine and others feminine. Different times and places reflect varying expectations, but one thing is certain: There are differences between men and women.

Theorist/sex researcher John Money claims, "When only three days old, girls have finer hearing, males more discriminating vision. Late in life males seem to depend more on visual sexual stimuli, females on verbal, auditory, and tactile stimuli."[7] If that theory is true, and I have no reason to doubt it, it correlates with what I consider to be God's pre-programmed differences between the sexes.

Although men and women have much in common, their sexual stimulation seems to come from different sources. Men are sexually stimulated by what they see, and that is why pornography is primarily supported by men. Women are stimulated by what they hear and read, and that is why the greeting card industry is primarily supported by women. The generalization that men give intimacy for sex and women give sex for intimacy is generally true.

The good news for women is that most men seem to change their attitude toward exploitative sex as they mature, realizing that there is more to sex than orgasms. Still, neither men nor women should apologize for or be embarrassed about their sexual needs. God gave us different needs, and we are drawn together to meet those needs.

Through a series of questions designed to outline preferred aspects of sex for 2,372 women, 22% preferred closeness or a feeling of oneness with their partner; 21% preferred orgasm; 20% preferred intercourse; 19% preferred foreplay; 9% preferred "everything"; 7% preferred oral-genital sex; and 2% gave other responses.[8] Although 22% represents a slim margin, most of the women surveyed "preferred closeness or a feeling of oneness with their partner" as a way to communicate love. Communicating as part of a sexual encounter was important to those women. That does not necessarily mean that a woman desires audible communication during sexual intercourse, nor does it mean that women require any other special kinds of communication. What that preference does suggest is that sex is more inclusive for women, perhaps even less physical, than for men. And, that is why communication—words, feelings, tenderness, symbols of affection in whatever form—are important to women.

Although the "Sexual Satisfaction Among Married Women" study did not rank preferences, it has been my observation, after years of discussion with couples on the topic, that most women would rank "preferred closeness or a feeling of oneness with their partner" far above any of the other categories. While men may minimize communication of feelings, women maximize communication even to the point where many of their sexual needs are satisfied by candid communication. Rare is the man who willingly substitutes talk for sex.

The man who realizes that his wife shows signs of starving for communication from him should also take note that communication could strengthen their relationship. Many counselors could attest that the majority of their clientele are women. From that it is possible to conclude, if tentatively, that women need a receptive ear and verbal encouragement.

What is your love language? Men are often the initiators in sexual activity, women the recipients.

The male has a profound urge to give, to woo his woman, to pursue, to initiate. His sexual organ, the penis, penetrates her body, and her vagina receives his ejaculation. How do those differences affect love language? If you, as husband and wife, desire to give each other sexual enjoyment, what can you do to meet the two kinds of sexual preference: the visual and the verbal? You both need some fantasy in your sexual relationship. You both need wooing. You both need loving, unselfish encouragement. You both need to hear the chimes ring. Think about that. What kinds of things could you do to bring back the romance in your marriage?

To give you just a little more understanding of the differences in attitude toward sex, let us consider the developmental process for a moment. By sixteen years of age, a male has just begun to experience his sexual peak, yet he (generally) does not fully understand his sexual drive. All he really knows is that he wants it satisfied. Fortunately for him, his sexual urges plateau by age fifteen and begin a slight decline by his mid- to late twenties. By then, his energy is focused more on his employment than on his sexual relationship. (To suit our purpose, we assume he is a married man by the time he is twenty-five or so.) Whether this emphasis on work over sex is due to a sense of responsibility to make a living or whether work becomes more appealing than sex as time goes by is difficult to determine. In either case, there seems to be a redirection toward sexual moderation, refinement and courtesy, which is a welcome relief to wives who in the past may have felt exploited.

Well, that is enough, for the moment, about men. At age sixteen, now, a female is far less interested in sex than are her boyfriends. She may use sexual suggestion to attract them. She may even accept sexual intercourse in spite of warnings and her own uneasy, almost subconscious feeling that no good will come of it, but not because sex is an end in itself. No, she will use sex to get something else: to hold onto a relationship or to feel included. When she becomes a married woman and ostensibly has what she used sex to gain, she may be criticized for not showing enough interest in sex or in her sexual partner.

For a woman, sex is usually less important than her other needs: her responsibilities with regard to her children, the home environment, her career. Then, at thirty-five or forty years of age, she sees that the soft, supple feel and curves of her youthful body are being replaced with wrinkles and folds, and her once boundless energy seems to have diminished. An instinct for renewed sexual activity takes over as if to compensate for her youthful charms, and her husband is delighted. Now more than ever she needs to experience sex, for to her it symbolizes her mate's loving desire for her even with the subtle changes of aging.

Maturity, after all, is more than aging. Maturity is an ever-growing compilation of experiences and understanding. In the process of maturation, a married couple will grow either closer or farther apart— closer by paying attention to each other, in generosity, farther by ignoring each other, in selfishness. Maturity should bring the profound revelation that two people have a need-oriented love; more, that the giving love they once considered an obligation has become natural and spontaneous. Spiritual maturity means growing more and more into the image of Christ. If a husband and wife are both becoming more like Him, following His biblical example, they can see Jesus' love in each other's eyes. When they make love, they make love *in* love, and sex becomes better and better. Maturing intimacy is continually enhanced, enriched and blessed of God. Few experiences could be any finer.

Do you not see, when you want to fulfill your partner sexually, you first need to put into practice all those elements that comprise Christlike love? When your attitude has become one of genuine, giving love, you will have accomplished something very important: You will have provided your mate with the basis for trust, the freedom to love you wholeheartedly, to give joyfully, with abandon, with the love that comes from a humble heart. What can you give your mate? What will make the chimes ring? Give your heart. Now, with the discovery or reminder of each other's needs, you have the opportunity to experience this ultimate in marital intimacy: sex as God meant it to be.

The Salvation/ Love Ratio

Salvation Is to Baptism What Love Is to Sex

*I*t is as clear to me as if it happened yesterday: raising my hand, walking nervously down the church aisle, kneeling and reciting words prompted by the evangelist. Even while watching others at the penitent rail, I received Jesus Christ as my Savior. Willingly I gave my life to Him—everything that I identified as me and mine, my past and my future. I gave it all to Him, and I desperately wanted Him to know everything about me. Little did I realize as a boy of five that I had taken on a life-long responsibility.

What I experienced was God's plan for reconciling me to Him through His only begotten Son, Jesus. That plan is called *salvation*. When I approached Christ for the gift of salvation, my soul was exposed to God. He saw everything. Nothing could be hidden from Him, absolutely nothing. He knew the bad as well as the good. Jesus knew everything about me, and yet He was willing to give me His redeeming forgiveness and incomparable, unconditional love. Because of His complete knowledge of me, I was vulnerable to Him, but down through the years He has honored my trust. He "does not change like shifting shadows" (James 1:17) although I can change my attitude toward Him. Nothing can come between us unless *I* allow it myself. Even when that happens, He knows about it, and He corrects, guides and loves me back into His will. His intimate relationship with me is evident all of the time.

There is no use trying to hide anything from Him. "God is greater than our hearts, and he knows everything" (I John 3:20). We cannot run away from Him because He is everywhere, continually reaffirming His love for us even though He knows our hidden ugliness, self-centeredness and pride. We are vulnerable, and no exposé ever written could reveal something about us that God does not already know. And why should we avoid Him? His is the only *unconditional* love to be found. "We love because he *first* loved us" (1 John 4:19).

As we learn how to behave as heirs of His Kingdom, we make mistakes and God's Holy Spirit works within us to help us correct them. Sometimes we deliberately disobey Him and have little reason to question why He disciplines us; if we were not His children, it wouldn't matter what we did. As He loves us, so we are to love Him and to live with an attitude of love toward others. "This is love: that we walk in obedience to his [God's] commands. As you have heard from the beginning, his command is that you walk in love" (II John 6).

Salvation is the greatest gift of love that you and I can receive, and it usually evokes the desire to offer our lives wholly to God in return. Baptism offers us that opportunity to show our love in a visible, tangible way.

While attending seminary, the people of a church north of Boston called me to be their pastor. It was there that I met Sharon Fowler, a ten-year-old daughter of one of the deacons. Oh, how I enjoyed getting to know that family of dedicated Christians! There was something special about them: While most people concerned themselves with their own interests, the Fowlers generously welcomed others into their hearts and showed true Christian concern for them.

As pastor of a small church, I did not often have the opportunity to conduct weddings, baby dedications and baptisms; but when I did, they were highlights of the year. The Fowlers had a growing family, and because of their obedient faith, many of the church ceremonies were centered around their children. Baptism was perhaps one of the most dramatic for two reasons. First, it was a public proof that a person identified himself or herself as a Christian. Second, it involved the preacher's standing in a slippery tank of cold water with a shivering baptismal candidate in front of a curious congregation dressed in their Sunday best and quite dry. How I managed to be formal and dignified in that setting I do not know, but baptism was an *event*.

I will never forget Sharon Fowler's baptism. Sharon was a celebrity for this brave and symbolic act for the simple reason that she was my very first baptismal candidate, and everyone in the church knew it. We were able to secure the use of a neighboring church's baptismal tank, and long hours went into preparation for the service. You would have thought it was a wedding, and indeed, it was just as important.

The Sunday afternoon arrived. There was a quiet expectancy as the little girl and I entered the baptistry. The water was cold, but that was not important. The floor of the tank was slippery, and I held onto Sharon to keep her from falling. Her trust in me and what I was about to do nearly overwhelmed me. I fought back tears of joy as I laid her into the waters of baptism and brought her up, symbolically a new creature in Christ. Only Sharon could see the tears in my eyes as I felt a vicarious identity with the Father in heaven. He wants to see in all of us the same childlike trust that Sharon had. Her baptism was an outward sign of the inward fact that she was already a child of God. Her trust came about *through* a relationship as a *result* of a relationship. It was the kind of trust that comes when people take the time for it to occur. And it does take time.

Salvation comes first, and then baptism.

$\dfrac{\text{Salvation}}{\text{Baptism}}$

Love and sex meet in another, parallel ratio of great importance. Like salvation and baptism, love and sex are based upon a relationship that takes time. And like baptism, sex must follow, not precede, love.

Love comes first, and then sex.

$\dfrac{\text{Love}}{\text{Sex}}$

Not everyone thinks so, though, at least not at first. A young couple told me about their courtship. With a cheery glow on their cheeks, they said it was a steamy one, but they also told me about the guilt they had felt. Both were looking for love and a marriage relationship. So, when mutual friends paired them up at a party, they made a too-quick decision. Before long, Donna was expecting a baby.

Fred's immediate reaction was, "Get an abortion. Do it now, before you think too much about it." He could not seem to come up with any other solution. But when he began to think of Donna's welfare, he realized that the baby was their child, not some *thing* that had happened to humiliate him and jeopardize his future. He had an adjustment to make. Until the news that Donna was pregnant, he had only himself to think about. Now he had two others. Were they freeloaders, or was he responsible for them? How could he trust Donna to really love him? Donna had the baby in her womb, a constant reminder of how her life had abruptly changed. She worried that Fred might leave her on her own if she did not get an abortion, yet she longed to keep her baby safe. How could she trust Fred to really love her?

Guilt feelings kept them from the abortion clinic. They could not cope with killing the baby and having that on their consciences. Somehow what had become their common problem brought Fred and Donna closer together emotionally, and soon after the baby was born, they were married.

The next few months were rugged. To Fred, they represented a series of pressures and failures. One day he sat in the back of a '78 Chevy pickup with a shotgun barrel pressed to his cheek, about to plaster himself to the truck bed. His boss kicked the butt end of his gun away from him, and dazed, Fred rolled off the truck tailgate into the arms of two paramedics and a police officer. They notified Donna, and she rushed to the hospital to be with him.

The issue had come to a head, and Fred was now ready to talk to Donna about it. She responded with loving concern. Those were their first real get-acquainted times. Every day of the two weeks that Fred was hospitalized for depression, Donna was with him, and their romance that had begun with lust and nearly ended with trauma and suicide, was turning into love. You see, Fred and Donna were fortunate enough to turn the ratio of *sex*/love into *love*/sex. In their crisis, they got to know each other and value what they learned. Most relationships in which sex is paramount disintegrate into bitter memories.

What is the signature of your home? Is it discord,

or is it harmony? You know now that you need to understand and trust each other before you can love freely and be freely loved in return. All twelve chapters of this book focus on this single, initial key: *knowledge*. The more you share of yourselves; the more time you spend together; the more you cultivate an attitude of caring, loving concern; and the more you follow Christ's example of self-giving love, the sooner you will learn the qualities that will nurture your marriage.

The joy, the warm and friendly glow, the blessing of kindred spirits, the security and the commitment that lasts for the duration take time and your personal investiture. What you *know* will determine how you can make your love grow. May the harmony of heaven be reflected in your home as you reach, not for the stars, but for each other.

NOTES

[1] "Tailor-made Pilot," *Flying*, Vol. 110, No. 2 (February / March 1983), pp. 14,15. Reprinted by permission of DCI, New York.

[2] Ancelle, "The Wall Between," *Discovered by Love* (Newman Press, 1967). Reprinted by permission of Paulist Press, Mahwah, New Jersey.

[3] Nick Stinnet, *Family Concerns*, Vol. 3, No. 6 (June 1986).

[4] Paul Tournier, *To Understand Each Other*, trans. John S. Gilmour. (Richmond, Va.: John Knox Press, 1968), p. 17.

[5] Roger Von Oech, "Sufi Judge," *A Whack on the Side of the Head* (New York: Warner Books, 1983), p. 23. Reprinted by permission of Warner Books.

[6] Florence Bienenfeld, "New Hope for Troubled Marriages," *Marriage and Family Living*, Vol. 62, No. 10 (October 1980), pp. 6-9. Concept used by permission of *Marriage and Family Living*.

[7] Milton Diamond and Arno Karlen, *Sexual Decisions* (Boston: Little, Brown and Company, 1980), p. 100.

[8] Robert R. Bell and Phyllis Bell, "Sexual Satisfaction Among Married Women," *Medical Aspects of Human Personality*, Vol. 1, No. 12 (December 1972), pp. 136-144.

Other Good Harvest House Reading

INTIMACY
The Longing of Every Human Heart
by *Terry Hershey*

Terry explains why we often simultaneously crave *and* fear intimacy, and how that draws us toward successive patterns of hurt and frustration—in friendships, dating, and marriage. More importantly, he tells us how we can experience balanced, healthy human relationships—by *first* establishing an intimate relationship with our Heavenly Father.

THE INTIMATE HUSBAND
by *Richard Furman*

The Intimate Husband is the account of one man's decision to regain the love of his wife and save his faltering marriage. Talking with successful husbands around the country, he found the tools to reestablish the intimacy God intended.

ROMANTIC LOVERS
The Intimate Marriage
by *David and Carole Hocking*

Here is romantic love for married couples that exceeds our greatest dreams and expectations! Greater intimacy is possible as we follow God's beautiful picture of marriage as found in the Song of Solomon.

GOOD MARRIAGES TAKE TIME
by *David and Carole Hocking*

Filled with teachings rooted in God's Word, this sensitive book offers help in four areas of married life: communication, sex, friends, and finances. Questions throughout the book for both husbands and wives to answer.

DATING YOUR MATE
by *Rick Bundschuh* and *Dave Gilbert*

If you've ever longed to return to those wonderful, fun-filled days of "courting," then *Dating Your Mate* is for you and your spouse. Chock-full of clever ideas that will put the romance, excitement, and spontaneity back in your life, *Dating Your Mate* is a practical guide to creative fun for marrieds and yet-to-be-marrieds. Delightfully illustrated by the authors.

ROMANCE REKINDLED
by *Rich Bundschuh and Dave Gilbert*

A book that is sure to reignite the embers of married romance. A virtual gold mine of practical ideas that will help you: get an unromantic spouse interested, write a great love letter, create that perfect mood; and dates that will keep your romance alive throughout the years. An exciting sequel to the bestselling book *Dating Your Mate*.

Dear Reader:

We would appreciate hearing from you regarding this Harvest House nonfiction book. It will enable us to continue to give you the best in Christian publishing.

1. What most influenced you to purchase *The Marriage You Always Wanted But Never Thought You Could Have*?
   - ☐ Author
   - ☐ Subject matter
   - ☐ Backcover copy
   - ☐ Recommendations
   - ☐ Cover/Title
   - ☐ _____

2. Where did you purchase this book?
   - ☐ Christian bookstore
   - ☐ General bookstore
   - ☐ Department store
   - ☐ Grocery store
   - ☐ Other

3. Your overall rating of this book:
   ☐ Excellent ☐ Very good ☐ Good ☐ Fair ☐ Poor

4. How likely would you be to purchase other books by this author?
   - ☐ Very likely
   - ☐ Somewhat likely
   - ☐ Not very likely
   - ☐ Not at all

5. What types of books most interest you?
   (check all that apply)
   - ☐ Women's Books
   - ☐ Marriage Books
   - ☐ Current Issues
   - ☐ Self Help/Psychology
   - ☐ Bible Studies
   - ☐ Fiction
   - ☐ Biographies
   - ☐ Children's Books
   - ☐ Youth Books
   - ☐ Other _____

6. Please check the box next to your age group.
   - ☐ Under 18
   - ☐ 18-24
   - ☐ 25-34
   - ☐ 35-44
   - ☐ 45-54
   - ☐ 55 and over

Mail to: Editorial Director
Harvest House Publishers
1075 Arrowsmith
Eugene, OR 97402

Name _____

Address _____

City _____ State _____ Zip _____

Thank you for helping us to help you in future publications!